SOUL
Surfing

SOUL
Surfing

TUNE IN YOUR POWER TO LIVE
THE MOVIE OF YOUR LIFE

Dawnea Adams

Delacorte Press

Published by
Delacorte Press
Bantam Doubleday Dell Publishing Group, Inc.
1540 Broadway
New York, New York 10036

The names and identifying characteristics of the individuals
counseled by the author have been changed to protect their privacy.

Library of Congress Cataloging in Publication Data
Adams, Dawnea.
Soul surfing : tune in your power to live the movie of
your life / by Dawnea Adams.
p.   cm.
ISBN 0-385-31933-9
1. Self-actualization—Miscellanea.   2. Visualization—
Miscellanea.   3. Parapsychology.   I. Title.
BF1045.S44A33   1998
153.3—dc21   97-29476
                                                         CIP

Manufactured in the United States of America
Published simultaneously in Canada

January 1998
10   9   8   7   6   5   4   3   2   1

BVG

FOR HEIDI

My daughter, my best friend.
Thank you for choosing me for a mom.

Special thanks to:

My dear friend Betty for keeping the faith.
My agent, Anne Sibbald: I am your Cuba Gooding, Jr.!
My editor, Tom Spain, for being the "other voice" that
    Divine Mind speaks through.
Barbara Hutnick for making my writing your Holy
    Grail.
Hilary Henkin for insisting I had the writing in me.
Dell Publishing for taking a chance with me.

Most of all, my love and thanks to every person I have
had the honor to work with. Bless you! Bless each and
every one of you. Because you opened up your heart to
my work, because you trusted, because you allowed
what works through me to touch your life, this book is
possible. I honor each of you with all my heart.

CONTENTS

SOUL
Surfing

A STAR IS BORN

You are standing on the edge of the abyss;
Everything your heart aches for is within your sight.
Behind you, the past is a stagnant landscape of compromise,
The now has led you to this place.
The fear of falling grips you like icy tendrils
As you shake your head, willing the terror away.
Ahh, a breeze of faith whispers over your soul.
You back up a few paces, and running with all your might,
You leap into the air!
You are the eagle that has taken flight;
Your eyes are riveted to what awaits you on the other side.
You land with both feet on the ground, running.
Tears stream down your face as you savor the sweet taste of victory.

"Faith and the Beast"
by Dawnea Adams

You. That's who I am talking about. You are about to become the star of the movie. What movie, you ask? The movie of your own life. The life you've only dared to dream about.

"If only I could . . ." How many times have you said that to yourself as you sat and stared off into space? Then you sigh, let go of the dream once again, and come back around to the "real world"—the office piled high with paperwork you don't want to do, or the home that's so small, you can hear the neighbors arguing, or the rush-hour traffic where you're stuck behind a van that's spewing toxic fumes all over your newly washed car.

Sound familiar? I know it does. People the world over have come to me for years for help living their dreams. They come to me because I have been given the gift of telepathy. I am known as a psychic, an intuitive counselor, healer, teacher, or whatever my clients want to call me. But I don't have to "read minds" to know what has brought you to this book. And you don't have to be "psychic" to find help in the pages that follow.

What if I told you that you can *live* what you sit and daydream about? Imagine how life would be if you could go through the day knowing you can get from that crowded office, home, or freeway to the place where your desires and your dreams become reality. A place where you write, produce, direct, star in, and—most important—*live* the movie of your life, a movie with the ending that you always wanted. That place already exists within you, and if you know how to find it, and what to do when you get there, you can make the movies of your mind come to life. You can accomplish everything you thought was out of reach, and live the life you thought could exist only in your mind. In fact, it's waiting for you in your soul, ready to be brought into the "real world." *Soul Surfing* will show you how.

Our world grows more complex, and often more frightening, with each passing day. No wonder you are searching, searching everywhere for answers. More important, you want to *know* that you can affect what happens in your life. You want to know there is something else besides the drama that plays itself out every day around you and in your life. You want to know there is a greater force you can put your faith in.

You are searching for that knowledge when you don't even realize it. You hear a song on the radio that touches you deep inside . . . ah, it sparks something. . . . Or you hear about a certain movie you *know* you must go see, and soon you're seated in that dark theater, waiting. . . . Or you pick up your remote control and begin "surfing" the television channels, or log on to your computer and "surf" the net . . . searching. . . . You scan the paper, the bookstores, looking for anything . . . anything to reaffirm that faith of yours that you *can* and *do* affect your own life. And that there exists a greater force that cares about you and about your life.

What you haven't realized is that all your wants, and all that you need, can be found inside yourself. Your soul is connected to that Divine loving force that *wants* you to have all that your heart desires. After all, if you weren't meant to have those desires become reality in your life, then you wouldn't feel that insistent urge to make them so.

It is really wondrous the way the mind and emotions can work together. You have a desire; your emotions allow you to feel that desire, and if you can picture it in your mind's eye, you're almost there. This work is about making *changes* in your life. It's about seeing the results those changes bring into your life. It's about *living* that inner dream. Soul surfing will help you live the dream every day of your life and much, much more—just like it has helped the thousands of people I have had the privilege to work with over the years.

In the chapters ahead, you will read about some of these people. I will share their stories with you. You will read about their struggles and victories, and how— through soul surfing—they changed their lives. You are no different from them. Those changes you are longing for can happen for you.

Nobody is holding you back but you. Don't feel bad— we all do it. We all get in our own way by focusing on the mental messages that prohibit our total expression— those "reruns" we play over and over in our minds that say, *You can't do it. . . . You can't have it. . . . You can't be it.* You know, the "Can't" Film Festival. You've been there, and I have too. They're the movies playing right next door to your dreams. But somehow, they seem more convincing, more real.

Not anymore. *Soul Surfing* will teach you how to zero in on the messages that hold you back and to change the channels once and for all. With the techniques of soul surfing you will travel "in between" the world in which you live and the world in which you dream, to reprogram the reruns you've been watching far too long. You will return from your inner world able to make your thoughts, dreams, and desires into reality—writing the happy ending (or new beginning) to the movie of your life.

Think of what happens when you go to the movies.

It's almost as if you're in two places at once—there in your seat, watching, and up there on the screen, living the drama of the movie. If it's a good movie, and your emotions are so swept up that you *become* the character you're watching, you are suspended between two worlds—the "now" world of you in the theater, and the world you're watching on the screen. But when it's all over, and you return to the "real" world, you're just a little bit different—because your emotions know that they've been somewhere else.

Soul surfing works the same way. You will journey to a world where that voice inside of you speaks freely of your hopes and dreams. Soul surfing will help you to turn up the volume on your inner voice; that timid little voice that once spoke in a whisper of desire will begin to roar—and you will love it!

Instead of allowing that timid little voice of the past to say, *I can't . . . I can't . . . I can't . . .* you will hear yourself roar, "Wait a minute . . . yes, I can." Your emotions will hear you too. And, like the emotional connections they make at the movies, they'll know it's true. You'll feel it—and believe it—long after the movie is over.

I want you to say this out loud now: "I can take back my power. Not only can I take it back, I *will* take my power back, right here, right now." Doesn't that feel good? God, I love this work!

I'll let you in on a big secret your own mind has been withholding from you: You have not lost your power. You have just allowed other people's voices, or your own fears, to play over and over inside your mind, so that the voice of your own power could not be heard. With soul surfing the voice of your soul, that part of you that is connected to the Divine Mind, is in charge. That is the voice you will listen to from now on! It has been patiently waiting for you. Welcome home!

Once this happens, anything is possible. In the pages ahead you will discover you have the power to reconnect with your creative spark, find your true life mate, and manifest the career you've only dared dream of. You will meet people like yourself who have used soul surfing in their lives to lose weight, pass crucial exams, get that promotion, and to communicate clearly their hearts' desires. Most important, you will finally be able to reclaim your heritage as a Child of the Divine, to live your life no longer in loneliness, in fear, in lack, but rather in total peace, total harmony, total joy.

Sound exciting? It is! Believe me, it is! How do I know it is? Everything you read in this book, every single thing I teach you, I have not only taught to others, but have done myself. I've lived it all myself—because before I could ever teach anyone to soul-surf, I had to learn it myself.

Every day people from every walk of life, from all over the world, call me or see me for guidance. Years ago, when I began this work, I used my telepathic abilities only to *guide* them, not *teach* them. Back then I *told* them what to do. In no time at all I realized that simply telling them wasn't enough. I needed to *show* them as well. That's where soul surfing helped me to help them.

I began to show my clients how to "get it" for themselves; not to wait for my predictions to happen, but to make them happen.

I use movies and music as tools in this book, because I love them. I also realize the power they have because I work with so many of the people in those industries who create those very movies and music scores that impact all of us every day. They are already at work in all of our lives; now, with soul surfing, you will learn how to put the power of movies and music to work for your dreams in ways you never thought possible.

I am sensitive to the healing powers that are available to us because I have known since I was a little girl that there was a greater force at work in my life. I have always known (though not always trusted *when* or *how* it would happen) that the day would come when I would bring the teachings that Spirit has brought to me—and through me—to you.

I want to share with you a life-changing event that happened to me when I was five years old when my father, an evangelist, took me to Angeles Temple for a "revival" service. As soon as I walked into the temple, I had the strongest feeling I'd been there before. I knew something was going to happen. It didn't take long for me to find out what it was. The woman onstage was preaching the "usual" hellfire-and-brimstone sermon I'd heard countless times. She stopped in midsentence, pointed to my father, and demanded he bring me up onstage. She rolled her eyes back in her head and proceeded to "prophesy" over me, saying that God told her

I was to be a great healer. That, one day, I would touch many lives.

Though I strongly disagreed with her, both at the time and through the years that followed, the time came for me to live out that preacher woman's prophecy.

My life has not been easy. I will share many of my most painful experiences with you in this book. Though it hurts to do so, I am willing to relive these gut-wrenching, faith-testing, frustrating times to show you those occasions when I broke through the pain and healed myself. Because if I can heal myself, with Divine help, of course, you can too. And more important, you don't have to be a telepath to soul-surf. Anyone can do it.

Since we're talking about making movies—the movies you make in your mind—let's look at how they make movies in the "real" world. There's a producer, who sets things up; a writer, who creates the script; a director, who puts it together; and actors, who, with the director's help, draw on their talents to bring it to life. Later on, of course, there's the audience, who bring it to life again—in the world "between" the world of the movie theater and the world on the screen (or the living room and the TV set, since most people also watch movies on video these days).

In the work you're about to learn, you perform all of these roles. Soul surfing involves the producer's "pre-production" preparation for your inner moviemaking, the writer's preparation of the script, and the director's decision on how your inner movie will be shot. The director in you will know how to get you, the actor (who will be up there on that giant screen in your mind), to use the latent talents you have: your intuition, imagination, and emotion, which, when connected by will to your spirit, create a powerful fusion within you that shapes the movie of your new life.

Whew, sounds like a lot of work, doesn't it? Filmmaking is. All pieces must be in place. Everyone must work together for the movie to be a success. Don't panic . . . soul surfing isn't as much work as filmmaking—you are the one in charge. Through soul surfing you will see how easy and fun it is to get all parts of you to work together. Then comes the long-overdue moment of exhilaration when you sit down and watch yourself on that giant screen in your mind. Even better, in this part of the process, called "phasing," you will *experience* those results you've worked for on that screen; they will be real in your life outside. Hey, Oscar night ain't got nothin' on you: the producer, the director, and the star of your own movie! The payoff is huge!!! You are literally living your dream.

The phases are the steps we take to surf our souls, the wind that carries us on the journey back "home." Like the Prodigal Son in the Bible, you will return home to the arms of the Divine Father/Mother, who will lovingly wrap you in the finest robes and prepare a feast in your honor. Everything you have been searching for— starving for—can be yours. I know this because I have taught the techniques of soul surfing and phasing to thousands of people the world over, and watched as their lives unfolded with satisfying results. More important, as I mentioned earlier, I can tell you that they've worked for me; everything I'll teach you or have used with a client was first tested out on me—by Divine Mind.

What I have learned is that soul surfing and its phases have been given to us by Divine Mind as a way to get back in touch with Divine power and love, by using the tools we were given long ago. Like filmmaking, soul surfing depends on many different pieces coming together. You'll see that movies play a role, as well as music. The most important tools come from within you: the gifts of imagination, intuition, and emotion, brought together by your will to create something within you so real that it actually takes place in your life. *You* do this. And, yes, it works!! Why? Because you are finally listening to that voice of your soul, the voice that wants joy, happiness, and abundance for you. By soul surfing you are giving that voice a place to become real, on that screen in your mind. That voice is your connection to Divine Mind, that loving part of the Universe that sees us as perfect in every way. Free of pain, free of lack, free of fear.

Let's talk about the word *intuition* for a moment. *Webster's* defines *intuition* as the power or faculty of attaining direct knowledge or cognition without evident rational thought and inference. Let me take it several paces further; the key to accessing your own intuitive ability is the *knowing,* beyond a shadow of a doubt, that what you are seeing, hearing, or feeling is real. As real as the room you are sitting in. As real as the air you breathe. You can't see the air, but you *know* it is real. You know it because you are breathing it. It's the same with intuition. Your intuition may also come to you through a strong feeling that, try as you might, you cannot dismiss. Or an inner voice prompting you to do something about a situation in your life, nagging at you until you listen. You've heard that voice, and you know that when you ignore it, you later regret it. Think of the times you've said to yourself that you should have followed your first mind, listened to your inner self, or gone with your gut. That was your intuition at work, expressing itself through your physical senses.

Everyone accesses their intuition differently. Some people either "feel," "hear," or "see" what they are intuiting; others, like myself, do all three simultaneously. But know this: You have it. Every person on this planet has it to some degree. The more you *trust* it, the more it will serve you. Intuition will assist you every day of your life. You can draw on it for making the large life-changing decisions that are so hard to make, and you can put it to use in matters as simple as being at the mall at holiday time and knowing that if you go three rows over you *will* find that parking spot. Until now you may not have known what to do with those intuitive feelings or hunches. Soul surfing will make you aware of the gift of your own intuition. With soul surfing and phasing you will use this powerful tool of "knowing" to work for you. You will use this process to create the life that your intuition has been guiding you to all along.

I use my telepathic gifts constantly. These gifts I draw on are from a greater source than myself. Every day before I begin working with my clients, be it on the telephone or in person, I ask Divine Mind to assist me in helping each person I come in contact with. I have been labeled many things over the years, the least of which is "psychic," a word whose connotations make me cringe—and I'm sure many of you as well. The word I use to describe my healing abilities is *telepathy*. That word describes how I see and do what I do: I draw energy from Divine Mind and transfer that energy to the person I am working with in the form of words or healing.

This is how that energy is transmitted from Divine Mind through me: I am blessed with the ability to "see" (in Technicolor) vivid pictures of the life of the person I am working with. I also "hear" a distinct voice speaking to me about the person I am working with, and I "feel" what the person is and has been feeling about their life. Through these "gifts" I am given information about their past, present, and future *possibilities* (let us not forget about the free human will). Through the power of touch, or "laying on of hands," I can also transfer energy to heal, not only emotionally, but physically as well. Now, with *Soul Surfing,* this transfer of healing energy is taking another new form. I've always demanded of Divine Mind and myself that if I were going to have a healing practice or write a book, the needs of those seeking me out for help, for guidance, would be fulfilled through Spirit. I have no doubt that Spirit is present in the work we'll do in the pages ahead.

I know if you are reading this book, you most likely have an opinion as to what being "psychic" is all about. If your impressions are not all that great, I don't blame you; my blood boils when I read certain books or see ads about the "psychic hot lines."

Guiding people's lives is serious business. This work is one of the most misunderstood and misused professions there is. Though I want to shatter your "psychic" misconceptions, and teach you how to use your own intuitive abilities in ways you never dreamed of, there is really nothing strange about using these gifts. The Bible says, ". . . your old men shall dream dreams, your young men shall see visions." (A word here—obviously, the guys that wrote the Bible weren't that keen about women. It doesn't mean women cannot do the same thing. I'm living proof!) So please, do not be afraid of the gifts the Divine has bestowed upon all of us. That "feeling" or that "voice" or "vision" is a gift. Listen to it.

When people book an appointment with me, they are usually in some sort of crisis. They have tried everything else and I am the last stop; they want answers and they want them now. At that time the furthest thing from their mind is the use of their own "tools." Damn it, they just want it fixed. They want to know that this horrible time will end and that they will get through it. You know how it is when you're sitting in that dark theater. Luke Skywalker is dangling by his feet in mid-air, one hand severed from his battle with Darth Vader;

it doesn't look like help is forthcoming anytime soon. Your stomach is in a knot, your hands are clammy. You think to yourself, *Come on, hurry up and save him.* (Fortunately, Princess Leia hears his telepathic call and turns the starship around to rescue him.)

It's the same thing with you. When you are searching or in crisis you just want an answer. You want to know that it will be okay, that sooner or later it will all work out. You want that starship to come.

This is your lucky day. Through soul surfing you will discover that it *will* be okay—and that YOU will work it out. You will be the star, producer, and director of your own personal movie. You will write the script, and by doing so you will take control of your life. Is that cool or what?!

Remember how the fictional moviemakers in the film *The Player* changed the ending of the movie they were making to up its ratings? You can do the same exact thing. Through **intuition** and **imagination** and **emotion,** called into action by that **will** of yours, you can change the possible outcome of your life to exactly what you want!!!

By now you've probably noticed how important I feel movies are to our everyday lives. Think about how many times you have been in a funk and dragged yourself to the movie theater or put on that favorite video at home. By the time the movie is halfway through, you've forgotten all about your problems. You get caught up in that drama on-screen. Through soul surfing you will learn how to *use* your own movies to get caught up in the drama you create to bring into your life whatever you feel is missing.

So . . . what are we waiting for? Let's get to work on *your* life!!!

Preproduction

As I said earlier, the movies you watch take a lot of work before the cameras roll. So will yours.

This is the nuts and bolts of soul surfing. All parts of you are going to join together to "shoot" the movie of your life. Using your **intuition,** your **imagination,** your **emotions,** and your **will,** you're going to live it on a giant screen in your mind. Just like you do when you're at the movies.

First of all, your **intuition** has led you to this book. Your intuition will be at the helm of every phasing exercise you do. When you surf that soul of yours, searching your memories to find those times in your life that need to be healed, your intuition will let you know which phasing journey you most need. It will lovingly guide you through shooting the movie of your life.

Using your **imagination,** you will create the *inner* movie.

Imagination is the creative juice that brings your movie to life. It is what lives deep inside you. It does not know it cannot be done. Imagination reaches past your subconscious mind and its programmed responses to life—you know, that little voice that says, *I can't do it. I can't do it at all.* Imagination says, *Yes, you can do it. Just go out there and go for it.*

Will says, *Do not stop, do not give up, you are nearly there, keep going!*

And your **emotions** connect you to what your imagination and intuition create. You know how it is when you go to the movies—and you get caught up in the story the moment the first image appears on that screen. You actually become part of what is going on up there. Why? Because all of your emotions are connected to what you are seeing and hearing. Whatever is happening up there on that screen becomes real to you; movie industry people call it the "suspension of disbelief." I love that, don't you? You literally become the character on that screen. Through your senses (i.e., seeing, hearing, and feeling), you are *living* what is going on up there. That's what I want you to do in the exercises I'm about to teach you. And the more you can connect with the phasing chapters, the stronger their effects will be both inside you and out.

Think about the last movie you got caught up in. Most of you couldn't tell the difference between real-life experience and what you were watching. The same is true with the movies you create in your mind's eye. What you might see on the movie screen or what your mind sees on the giant screen in your imagination are one and the same. As long as you are connected emotionally, *it will work*!

As soon as the movie starts to roll, your emotions connect to what you see up there on that giant screen.

The same thing happens with your inner screen. Your emotions will "connect" to what you see and make it real inside of you, and in very little time, you will be living the results in your life.

Your **intuition, imagination, emotions,** and **will** are all you need to start creating your new life. The life you have always hoped for and dreamed of is on that giant movie screen inside of you, inside of your soul now. You are going to find it and let it out. Let it live in your life outside that screen in your mind. Actually, it's been right inside of you all along. Now you're going to let it out. Like when you were a little kid and you used to play make-believe. Remember?

DESTINY TURNS ON THE RADIO

*If you do not enter the
kingdom of heaven as a
little child, you will not go there.*

The Master Jesus

When I was a little girl, listening to my father preaching his sermons of sin and damnation, beads of sweat would pop out on the back of my neck, and my throat would go dry and my hands would get clammy. *Oh, no!* I silently cried as I panicked. *This is it—I'm going to hell!*

I thought he meant that Jesus was saying that if I didn't "get saved"—right then, right there—I wouldn't go to heaven. Only years later, when I started working with people in healing and counseling sessions, did I comprehend what that scripture meant.

When we are children, it is easy to live out our destiny. It is inside of us, a real part of ourselves. We have that innocent childlike faith in ourselves and the world around us. We have not yet learned it *can't* be done.

All of us come into this life with something we have chosen to do. I call it the "Chosen Destiny." You have one, too, and it is written on your soul, the part of you that was created from Divine Mind. (Call it what you like: God, the Goddess, Buddha, Muhammad, the Master Jesus, the Eternal Flame, the omnipresent source. Just call it. It's there and it wants to help you.) Your soul holds the memory of every life you have ever lived, every path you have traveled, every deed you have ever done. It knows every single thing about you. Don't be scared. It loves you, and it is there to help you!

Picture this: A gathering of spirits on what some people call "the other side." There's your soul, deciding if you should come back to earth and give it another shot. You meet with your committee of teachers and guides who keep an eye on your progress down here on good old earth—sometimes also lending a helping hand or a good swift kick in the rear when you need it. Today you and your committee are sitting in a theater, eyes glued to a giant movie screen. On that screen is your previous life on earth—in vivid Technicolor detail. You see where you passed with flying colors, where you did so-so, and where . . . hmm—mm, you failed miserably. When the movie ends, you sit there with the committee, reviewing all you just saw on that screen. You take a deep breath and say, "Okay, I'm ready to try again."

Then you and the committee decide what unique talents you will bring with you and what challenges you will face. This combination of talents and circumstances will give you the foundation to meet and rise above those challenges—to "rise to the occasion," so to speak, of your Chosen Destiny. Think about that word *chosen* for a moment. That means you are born with talents and abilities you *chose* to come back with. You are born with dreams you *chose* to fulfill. You don't have to suffer for those talents; you don't have to beg for those dreams to materialize. Everything you need to succeed at what you ache to do in this life already exists inside of you! It's been there from the beginning, and it's still there today!!! All you have to do is ignite it.

Each one of us has what it takes to ignite that Chosen Destiny—the Divine Spark. It lives and breathes in every person alive on this planet. The Divine Spark is the breath of Spirit that softly blows at the dying embers of your shattered dreams and brings them back to life.

I would like to share with you an example of Divine Spark. For many reasons I strongly fought living my Chosen Destiny. (You have, too, or your intuition would not have led you to this book.) My daddy is an evangelist. I've known I was a telepath since I was, maybe, three or four years old. So Daddy and I never saw eye-to-eye on the things he taught his following. He would preach that we're going to die and go to hell if we don't get saved. I never understood how a loving Father, God, could do that to His children. I used to blurt this out to him on the way home from church. You can imagine the reaction I got!

I stuffed down what I knew: the fact that I *was* a healer; that it was my Chosen Destiny to *be* a healer. I turned my back and ran. And Spirit allowed me to continue running for quite a few years. At one of the darkest times of my life, my latest attempt to run had taken me to Puerto Vallarta, Mexico, where I went into a little café for a bite to eat. At the entrance near the register was an exchange bookstore. I was standing in front of a row of tattered used books when *Illusions* by Richard Bach literally fell out of the shelf and landed on my bare toes. (Ouch!)

I had come across *Illusions* at a friend's house at another dark time—the onset of my divorce from my first husband, when I had randomly opened the book to a page that said, "There is no such thing as a problem without a gift in its hands. You seek the problems because you need their gifts." Well, let me just tell you, I slammed the book shut, rolled my eyes, smirked, and said, "Yeah, right." So much for listening to my intuition.

So when that book fell off the shelf and onto my bare toes, I figured there was something in there that I just might need to know. There was, and this time I was ready to hear it. Reading *Illusions* changed my life. It gave me the courage to live my Chosen Destiny. That's the way Divine Spark works. It will sweep its loving way into your life when you most need reminding that you are way off the path. It fans the spark to ignite the fire within you. Like I said before: sometimes so gently that you miss it, sometimes with a good kick in the rear!

The Chosen Destiny is that burning thing inside you. It is the thing you desperately wanted to be, and played at being, when you were a little kid. Remember saying, "When I grow up, I'm going to be . . ."? You would spend hours making believe that you were that person. Maybe you would pretend you were a singer, a dancer, or a musician. Or maybe you would take grand voyages across oceans you'd never seen, except in your imagination. Maybe you played at being mommies or daddies. Or, maybe, you just pretended you belonged to another family (where you were loved and accepted) because being in your own family was too painful. The Chosen Destiny was something you held deep inside. It made you feel like you could fly. It made you feel like you belonged; made you *feel* important. It was a place inside that knew, no matter where you were, you belonged. It grabbed your heart and made it sing.

Remember when you made believe how free you felt? Or how much emotion was tied in to those make-believe times? How much you felt you belonged in that place—a place that was as real to you as the world outside? Those were magical times. What felt like a living, breathing part of you was the voice of your Chosen Destiny expressing itself through you. And the love that fueled it, from that bonding of your emotions to that greater force within you, was the Divine Spark.

No matter what background you came from, or what your childhood was like, I'm sure you played this game—I know I did. But, as children, it wasn't a game; it was real. You didn't know otherwise. You were in total trust with yourself; you were in direct communication with your Divine Spark. Some of you spoke to it directly in the form of "invisible friends." For others it was a feeling—a wonderful love-filled emotion—that made you want to throw your arms around yourself, and out to the world, and love it with all you had inside you.

More important, the Divine Spark was a safe haven to

run to when the world outside you didn't believe. It was always there, even if the rest of the world let you down.

Then along came the "Conditioned Destiny." But the Conditioned Destiny is radically different. Why? Because the Conditioned Destiny is learned. It is not spontaneous; it comes from programming. It is composed of deeply ingrained messages that came to you from the world outside your minds, outside your hearts; the world outside your joy, your freedom, your love.

Every one of you had great teachers for this Conditioned Destiny: your families, peers, even schoolteachers. For some of you it was the church you attended—where you learned that God was an angry old man to be feared. Conditioned Destiny was the world outside. And that world had a much bigger voice. Your Conditioned Destiny stated, "No, there's only one way to do this, one way to live life, and, by God, you'll live it the right way—our way. And if you want our love, our support, our validation, you have to do it *our* way."

And when you resisted, you would hear, "Who do you think you are? You'll never amount to anything. Better listen to me, if you want anything in this life!" Or your Conditioned Destiny was the hand that came crashing down across your face, as the person wielding the blow looked at you with eyes swollen with anger and rage. Or it was: "If you love me, you'll see it my way, do it my way." Sound familiar? *Feel* familiar?

In other words, you learned quickly to bury that "chosen" part of yourself. You learned to bury it because you had no choice. You had to survive in this world—your world.

Little by little, for most of you the Chosen Destiny got pushed aside to make way for the Conditioned Destiny. While the Divine Spark still lived and breathed within you, you stopped allowing yourselves to listen to it, or feel it. You really had no choice. As a child you were forced to take the path of least resistance.

At the same time the Chosen Destiny—that part of you that knew the freedom and joy that came from pretending to be who, in fact, you really were—got buried deep inside you. What's worse, the joy of communication with the Divine Spark got buried with it.

(I think that's how Adam and Eve must have felt after being tossed from the Garden of Eden. Like them we took a big bite out of the apple. Life, that is; life here on earth.)

Over the years I have worked with so many wonderful people and I have watched in amazement as "the Work" unfolds miracles in their lives. I have seen breakthroughs in workshops and seminars. I have seen physical and emotional miracles in my treatment room. And for others it's a slower process; but it still happens—and when it does, it makes my heart soar for them.

Most of my work has been one-on-one; however, there was a time many years ago when I conducted seminars. That was the first time I used the term *phase.* (Though I had been doing and teaching the phasing process since I was a little girl.) This is the process you will learn in this book. You will use it to act upon those answers we find within ourselves by soul surfing, thereby creating the healing in our lives. I saw many people touched and healed in those evenings, in which I taught people how to go deep within to find answers and create healing in their lives. As rewarding as those evenings were, I didn't feel the time was right back then to bring the "teachings" to a public audience.

More important, I felt a tremendous obligation to my private practice, so I concentrated on my one-on-one, in-depth sessions. That's where soul surfing and phasing really blossomed. Now I am bringing them to you—and I cannot begin to tell you how excited I feel about sharing all of this with you!

On our journey together along the way, I will be sharing with you stories about the lives of some of these courageous people. I have changed their names and some of the circumstances to protect their privacy. I haven't changed anything about the experiences I've written about myself, however. You will be reading more about me in each phase—remember, even though I'm a telepath, I am human, just like you. If I can learn to do this, you definitely can learn it too.

I can't expect you to embrace your Chosen Destiny without telling you how I did. Here's how I finally stopped running and started living my Chosen Destiny.

When I came back from Mexico, I lost almost everything in my divorce. Yes, I *verbally* agreed to live my

Chosen Destiny and become a full-time healer. But when it got down to it, the voice of my Conditioned Destiny kicked in, saying, *Come on now, girl, you've got two kids to feed. No one knows who you are. How do you propose to make a living being a telepath?* Of course, fear took over; I grabbed the local paper, scanning it for a "real job." When I walked into the woman's office who was to interview me for said "real job" that next day, I began to tell her about herself. I could not keep my mouth shut. The words just poured out. Forty-five minutes later she looked at me with teary eyes, saying she could not, in all good conscience, hire me for the position. I was, after all, a healer. Look what I'd just done for her. (Ah, do you see the Divine Spark at work here?)

I left her office in a huff, mumbling under my breath. How was I supposed to feed my kids? I had less than five dollars to my name. I pulled into a Ralph's Market in the San Fernando Valley, still mumbling. Once in the store I headed for the cream of chicken soup, noodles, and tuna—the makings of my famous tuna casserole. As I stood in the checkout line, thumbing through the *National Enquirer,* the hair on the back of my neck stood on end. The man standing behind me clearly had heart problems. Never before had I approached a stranger about their life, and here I was stepping up to the plate *twice* in one day. Divine Spark was definitely at work here.

As I asked him about his heart problems, his face turned white as a sheet. He blurted, "How could you possibly know that?"

I shrugged, suggesting he see a doctor for medication and further stating that even though he feared it, he would *not* die at the same age as his father. His eyebrows shot up as he shook his head in silent agreement.

The woman in front of me in the checkout line asked, "Are you a psychic?"

I retorted, "No, I am a telepath."

She waved her hand, stating, "Whatever you want to call it, I heard what you said to that man. I am a psychic and I'm conducting a psychic fair this Sunday. Would you work it?"

I guess she could see the hesitation on my face. She went right on: "You get five dollars cash for each 'reading' you do."

There I was, holding the last five dollars to my name. What could I say? Scared shitless, I agreed to work. That's where my "Work" started. To this day that first experience with "the public" is a blur. All I know is that once the first person sat down in front of me, the people didn't stop coming the entire eight hours.

You know the feeling you get when you are exhausted and elated at the same time? That's how I felt. I knew. I knew I had stepped into my Chosen Destiny and there would be no looking back.

Through my work I have seen people come to me frightened, lost, and confused. I have watched them as they fought their inner battles and won. They have gotten past their conditioning to touch and ignite the Divine Spark within them, and in doing so they have changed their lives. That is what soul surfing is going to do for you. You will reconnect with your Divine Spark. That spark will give you the insight and courage to heal your past, to look at your life in the now, and to soar into your future. To claim your Divine birthright, which is freedom, happiness, abundance, and love.

In keeping with the words of Richard Bach, "We teach best what we need to learn," I am also on my life's journey. I am learning right along with you.

Part of soul surfing is creating an environment you can work in. Just like the people who go off on location to shoot a film, or do it on a soundstage somewhere, you will create an environment for yourself where you can work on *your* movie. In other words, it means spending time with yourself. Be it a few moments, a week, a month—or as long as you need—you will take the time to look at your life: the present (the life you have created today); and the past (the experiences that created the "today" in your life).

I will help you create that environment and then guide you through the ten different phases in this book; there's also a troubleshooting guide at the end. Each phase will teach you how to surf your soul and look "in between" the life you are living to find answers to specific problems. That is, to look past the present conditions in your life; to look deep inside yourself for answers; and to trust that "the Voice" that is speaking to you is the same one that speaks to me, because it is. Remember, we are in this together.

The Bible says, "Faith is the substance of things hoped for, the evidence of things not seen." In Bach's book *Illusions* Donald calls faith "imagination." I think *both* are correct. Both definitions, used together, create that part of us that *knows* we can "move mountains" in our lives if we really have the desire. The Divine Spark, or your intuition, feeds faith. Faith and imagination reconnect us to our Chosen Destiny.

Remember what I said earlier about spending time *within* yourself? Phasing will not deter you from living your day-to-day life; in fact, I've done it quite successfully driving down the freeway in rush-hour traffic, although I'm not recommending that you do so. It will not deter you from your job, family, friends, or the life you are living at the moment. But phasing will change your life—the way you *feel*, deep inside, it needs to be changed.

Why? Because you will have a new vision, a new opinion, a new feeling of yourself. You will take back your power. And once you have it back, and know how incredible it feels—like running down the street and clicking your heels together—you will keep it. Nothing and no one will ever be able to rob you of it again!

I've told you that phasing takes you "in between" worlds. That's where the growth takes place too. You will keep living in the life you have already created while you are changing that life. The change occurs in the time during which you are reconstructing your life, yet living your life in the day-to-day. Sounds a little weird, but it works.

The amount of time you invest in phasing depends on you. Let me say right here: more time is *not* necessarily better. It is *how* you spend the time that counts. Remember the magic words? **Intuition, imagination, emotion.**

Bring them willfully to bear on the ten phases in this book and you will feel yourself soaring high above your world. You will learn how to live in your world and keep your Divine Spark alive! And that Divine Spark will fan the flames of desire to reignite your Chosen Destiny.

Your Divine Spark is part of a much greater force. That force is love, and it carries the acceptance of all your hopes, of all your dreams. It knows that you are unique unto yourself. There is only one precious you on this planet, and you are meant to live your life as if each moment is precious—because it is. No matter what you've heard or read before this, no matter what you think your conditioning is, today is the day to claim your power and reignite the Chosen Destiny within you.

Setting Up the Scene

Let's get busy!!

There are several ways to use the ten steps of phasing. First things first.

I'd like you to read the entire book, each phase. As you are reading, your intuition will tell you which phase you need to work on first. Once you have decided which phase is the winner, read it through. Read it at least three times. Then get up and move around, get in your car and go for a drive, take a walk, do your laundry (all things I do when I am phasing). In other words, let it soak in.

I want all parts of you "hooked in" before you actually begin to phase. In connection with each phase is a movie that relates to the phase you are going to use. Most of you have a VCR; if not, use a friend's. That's right, get aggressive. Call them up, tell them you are coming over with a great movie, offer to make them dinner or bring them pizza. Put the movie on and let it sweep you away.

There is one more important thing to cover: music. I believe the Divine Creator created musical chords before anything else. I believe that because I have seen how deeply music touches every living thing. From plants, to humans, to all of the Universe. Remember *Close Encounters of the Third Kind*?

Many of us don't realize how important music is to all of us. Right now I want you to think of a song that you loved at some point in your life. Doesn't thinking of it take you right back to that time of your life? You bet your ass it does. You are back there living that moment as soon as you hear the first few chords.

To this day I cannot listen to "Hey Jude" by the Beatles without getting nauseous. I was pregnant with my first child when that song was popular. My now ex-husband played the grooves off that record, and to this day, every time I hear it, I get morning sickness. And that was twenty-seven years ago!

I have this running debate with myself about what influences us more—music, movies, television, or books. (Though I have to say that there is less and less a desire for most people to read in this instant-gratification world, and shame on us for that!)

All of these genres are pretty powerful. Look at Oprah Winfrey and how much she has helped people with her show. It's mind boggling how all of this affects us. From the clothes we wear, to the bodies we *think* we need to have, to the way we talk, walk, dress, think. I want you to learn to use these things to benefit your life. They are tools, powerful ones. Why? Because they capture the big three: **intuition, imagination,** and **emotion.** And they make your **will** say, "Get off your rear, get up, and get going!"

Back to the music. Take a moment. You are preparing to phase. Which phase has your intuition led you to? Using your intuition once again, choose songs that will assist you to *emotionally* tap into the feeling of that phase. When you are watching a movie, the background music plays a powerful part in connecting you to the emotion of a scene. I want you to do the exact same thing here. Carefully choose your musical score. It will greatly assist you to get your emotions to really connect to what you are seeing on that giant screen in your mind.

You are preparing to "shoot" your movie, but you aren't shooting it yet. Patience, patience.

Put the music on, sit down in a comfortable chair, close your eyes, and let it take you for a ride. What we are doing here is "revving" up, getting your emotions moving. I don't care if you listen to rap, rock, R & B, or Bach. Whatever floats your boat—put it on and do it!

I love the band U2. I think Bono is one of the most charismatic male performers I have ever seen. Something is definitely "coming through him" when he is onstage. Maybe it's that Celtic blood. Whenever I want to get revved up, I do "a double." I put U2's video "Rattle and Hum" in my VCR. I turn up the volume, and away I go. Not only do I hear the band, I see them as well. Just like at the movies. Only, at home I can dance around my living room. Halfway through I'm ready to rock. Whatever fear or stress I might have is gone! It's a double whammy to my emotions. Why do you think MTV has been so successful?

If I want to feel mellow, I put on some Aretha Franklin. See what I mean? Use the tools filmmakers have been using to nail you—the viewing audience—for years.

Okay, by now anticipation should be building. Let's get the props in place and roll the camera!!!

Your **imagination, intuition,** and **emotions** are revved!

Your intuition has chosen which phase you are to use.

Your **will** is ready to forge ahead.

Let's find the location and let the camera roll!!!

* * *

There are three locations to successful phasing I've found to be most effective.

Location #1: In this location you and your impressions of the phase you are using are what will feed the "you" up there on that giant screen in your mind's eye. Don't get nervous—it's not necessary to memorize the phase; your intuition will "pick up" on the key phrases and their powerful meaning. However, in order to use this technique effectively, you must thoroughly read the phase. And you must not only *read* the phase, you must *feel* it, as if you were reading a good book you can't put down. You want to keep reading, because you are so locked in to the story.

You must connect your emotions to what you are reading *before* you ever begin phasing. This is where you block out all other thoughts except for the journey that particular phase is taking you on. It is especially important here. You are using your own mind (and the mood you have set). When you close your eyes, you can see, hear, and feel what you are phasing.

Here are a couple of suggestions for this technique that will bring fantastic results. They've worked great for my clients, not to mention my daughter Heidi and me.

Actually, this is a lot of fun because you get to use the "artistic" part of you.

Make some small note cards or buy the $3^{1}/_{2}'' \times 5''$ size. On each card put a color, a picture, or a word that you feel will help you "key in to" the phase. Put the cards in

front of you. As you pick each one up, feel how you respond to it. It's as if you are already inside of the phase, or the phase is now living and breathing inside of you.

The other really cool thing to do is buy a piece of poster board. On the top of the board write "My Phasing Movie."

Then get creative. Draw a movie set on the board; place pictures you've either cut out of a magazine that "key in to" your phasing movie or draw them. Use paint, markers, glitter, crayons—get wild!!!

Not only is it great fun, it uses your creativity, and more important, it reinforces in you your belief that phasing works. Why? Because you've made the effort to create this wonderful movie.

While you are working on that particular phase, keep the "movie set" where you can see it at all times: in the room with you while you are phasing; in your bedroom—so it's the first thing you see when you wake up in the morning, and the last thing you see before you go to sleep at night. Pretty soon, all those little pictures, or words, or whatever you've put on that movie set, will start to find their way into your life.

At the beginning of every new year Heidi and I make this our little project. We put the new year on the top of our poster board. Then we put everything we want or want to happen for that coming year on our "set." Heidi is such a great "phaser." Last year, within a matter of a few months, everything she put on her "set" was in her life.

Okay, enough of the prep work, you are ready to phase. You've tapped into all parts of yourself. You are totally connected to the "knowing" this will work. And you have lined up your musical score. Have you ever seen a movie without one? Why should yours be different?

The music you have chosen for your musical score is mood-setting music. It doesn't distract you from phasing, it sets the mood. I love Suzanne Ciani when I soul-surf—especially her *Velocity of Love* CD. I don't think Led Zeppelin will work here, but if it doesn't distract you from connecting to that big screen in your mind, go ahead and use it. The point is this: I want you focused on the screen in your mind, not distracted by the music. It is important to remember that the setting is meant to enhance, *not* detract.

Put on your music and lower the lights. Candlelight is perfect for phasing.

Sit in a comfortable chair. *Do not* lie down. I don't want you sleeping on the set!! Sit comfortably erect, feet flat on floor, hands resting on knees, palms upward.

Now begin to breathe. In through your nose, out through your mouth. Why, you say? When you come out of your mother's womb, when you are still perfectly in touch with your Chosen Destiny, what is the first thing that you do? That's right, you breathe. The most important thing to remember before you start each phase is to breathe deeply. Now close your eyes, take a deep breath in through your nose. Shallow breathing will get you nowhere. You have to breathe deep down into your gut. So try again. Let all of your breath out through your mouth.

Now take a long . . . slow . . . deep . . . breath through your nose . . . hold it to the count of seven and let it out *hard* through your mouth. Okay, do it again—in through your nose, deep breath, hold it. Count . . . one . . . two . . . three . . . four . . . five . . . six . . . and seven. Now push your breath out of your mouth. Good, you're getting it.

Do this seven times exactly the same way. If you've done it correctly, you will feel relaxed, deeply relaxed. Incidentally, this works great when you're stuck in traffic, or your boss has just jumped down your throat for no reason. Or the kids in the next room are threatening to kill each other. It is an instant destresser.

You've worked really hard to prepare yourself. Congratulations, you are ready to "shoot" your movie.

Location #2: Repeat setting the mood and music as in Location #1. Do your circular breathing.

Record yourself reading the phasing exercise aloud on a blank cassette, set to your musical score, of course. You want to set up the scene and create the mood—just like in Location #1. Complete your circular breathing. Then, on the release of the seventh breath, press the play button on your tape recorder, close your eyes, and the giant screen in your mind will appear before you. As you listen to the tape of your own voice guiding you through the exercise, sit back and watch the show.

Location #3: Repeat setting the mood, the music, and the circular breathing you've read about in Locations #1 and #2.

You and a friend become phasing partners. One of you sits in the chair ready to phase, the other sits directly across from you. When you've finished your circular breathing, have your friend read the phase to you.

All of these locations work. Find the one that works best for you and use it!!!

SCENE IS SET, YOU'RE READY TO ROLL. . . .

You, the director, yell, "ROLLING!!!"

Okay, you can whisper if you want.

Edit

As soon as you have finished phasing, write down all of your impressions. What you *saw, felt,* and *experienced.* This is very important. You will be logging in as much detail as possible in your journal. (I don't care if you use paper towels to write on, as soon as your mind or your partner's voice yells, "Cut," you write down everything. If you want to keep a fancy journal, that's okay too. The point is, no excuses, just write it down.)

This helps you to really lock in your "phasing" experience. Keep going over and over the phase until you can feel it, see it, hear it. Every time you think about it, it's right there—even in your sleep.

Have I thought of everything? Oh, yeah, one more thing . . . Let's do it! Let's Rock and Roll!!

Off to the Movies

*Each journey
begins
with the first
step.*

Chinese Proverb
Anonymous

Phase One will introduce you to a part of yourself that is trapped inside of all your past conditioning: the conditioning from voices connected to your Conditioned Destiny.

This phase will take you "between worlds." It will put you in touch with the power that lies deep inside of you.

See a giant screen in front of you. You're looking at this giant screen, waiting for the movie to start. (At this point you may be feeling a little nervous; don't worry, it's perfectly natural.)

Suddenly, on the screen in front of you appears a ball of tangled string. Look carefully at it for a moment. It's large enough for you to see the layers and layers of the tangled mass of string. As you look closer, you can see the loose end of the ball of string. It's about eight inches long. As soon as you see it, use your mind and watch it start to slowly unravel. As it does, you begin to feel yourself unwind. Slowly, you feel yourself letting go. As you continue your breathing, feel yourself let go of all of your doubts, your fears, your frustrations, concerning your daily life. Continue to watch the ball of string unwind until it is completely unraveled. Be aware of how your body and your emotions are responding to this picture on the screen in front of you. Keep watching until the ball of tangled string is completely unraveled. As it gets down to the last remnants, you realize something is at the core of that mass of string. It is a tiny figure huddled in a ball. Look closely at that tiny figure. Concentrate on that small figure. It is you. The you that is locked inside of your life right at this moment. Your emotions have started to come up more fully by now. Let them! Feel their power flow through you.

As you acknowledge this realization, a soft radiant light shines down on that tiny figure on the giant screen.

It's like the light that shines through the trees in the forest, and it is filled with warmth, with love. Your soul is what you are seeing on the giant screen as it is being touched by the Divine Spark.

Take as long as you need. If the tears are building, let them flow. Let the light fill up all of you, until you feel that you have merged with the Divine Spark, merged with the love. Throw your arms open wide, turn your face upward, and bask in that beautiful light. See yourself as you are, right at this moment of your life on that giant screen. See yourself filled with that Divine light, that Divine love.

Now allow the screen to disappear. Be aware of the feeling

of warmth within yourself. Be aware of how, in these few moments, you have opened—you are in sync with the Divine Spark and are now able to trust. Take one last, deep breath; let it out, then open your eyes.

CUT . . . PRINT IT!

Right on! You are phasing. How does it feel?

Congratulate yourself!!

EDIT IT! Immediately write down all you saw, felt, and experienced.

Remember in the movie *Pretty Woman,* when Julia Roberts makes Richard Gere take the day off from work?

You see the two of them together in the park. Julia takes Richard's shoes off, takes away his cellular phone. They are lying on the grass, reading together. He looked totally at peace, didn't he?

For Richard's character, Edward, it wasn't about money, it wasn't about power. It was about allowing himself to be nurtured. Nurtured and loved. That was his Divine Spark. What's yours?

And for Julia? Well, all of us who saw that movie, over and over, know: She got the fairy tale. Her Divine Spark was moving out of a life she had been trapped in because of circumstances, into a life she'd belonged in from the beginning. Remember, she did not compromise. She did not accept the condo. She wanted it all, and in that moment of refusing to settle, she got it all!

The same goes for you. You do not want a half-life. You want it all!

This phase came to me when I was sixteen years old and far away from any feeling of love or acceptance. I didn't see much of my natural mother when I was growing up. From what my grandmother told me, my mother left me on her doorstep when I was two years old. I was shuttled back and forth between my grandmother and my father, and once was sent to an uncle in Nebraska. My grandmother is the only person in my childhood I recall caring about me. I constantly lived in terror of the day Daddy would come drag me out of school and take me away. When I was eight, the battle ended. He took me from school, telling me I would be living with him from then on. I cried myself to sleep for a week, begging him to let me go back to Grandma's. I knew if I cried I would get a beating, but I didn't care. My grandmother's was the only love I ever knew.

My parents parted ways when I was about two. My father remarried—the daughter of a preacher. That's when my father decided to become a preacher. That's when I got my first introduction to "religion." Revival meetings, that is. Hellfire and brimstone. It was also when I realized I could "see" things others couldn't. When I mentioned this to my stepmother, she said, "That's the devil talking," and proceeded to beat me. Many beatings by my stepmother, too many beatings, took place over those years from eight until I was thirteen. When I hit adolescence, the Scorpio in me kicked in. I refused to take the abuse anymore. I ran away from home. For a brief time (three months) I went to live with my mother. That's where I met the man who would become my first husband and the father of my two daughters.

As soon as my father heard about this, he came and got me. I'll never forget driving away from my mother's house, watching Gene wave good-bye from the sidewalk. Something inside of me just cracked. I told my father he could not keep me away from Gene, that I loved him. I remember my father's face in the rearview mirror as he said, "We'll just see about that."

I kept running away. They put me in a foster home for a while. Gene came to visit me there and I ran away with him to Las Vegas. We were under the insane assumption we could get married. What can I say? I was a kid.

My father and stepmother picked me up at the Las Vegas juvenile hall. It was the day after the Watts riots. I slept most of the way back. I thought I was going home. I wasn't. I opened my eyes to find myself outside of L.A. juvenile hall. I looked incredulously at my father and asked what I was doing there. He was dead silent as he led the way to the lockup. Once inside that buzzing metal door, I looked out of the little wire-meshed glass window at my father. He didn't look back. He strode out of there, and never once looked back.

What I could tell you about this time of my life could fill a book. It was quite a learning experience. I went from L.A. "juvie" to Los Padrinos, a place they put you until the court and your parents decide what to do with you. Then to Las Palmas, a maximum security lockup. They had decided—my father, my probation officer, and the judge, that is—that I was a runaway. *Only* a runaway. No drugs, no alcohol. (Looking back, there is no doubt in my mind it was a case of "money talks." In his own right my father was a very successful and very powerful man, and I had gone against his will. I believe he wanted me to know his will was law—kind of like the God he believed in.)

I graduated from high school at Las Palmas "school for girls." But it wasn't all bad: While I was in Las Palmas, the girls used to come to me, hoping I could help them with their problems. No small wonder, huh?

One night, shortly after arriving at Las Palmas, I was lying in my bed. I knew I was trapped. I was sixteen years old and I knew I would not get out of there until I turned eighteen. I cried and I cried and I cried. Then something deep inside of me reached out. I "saw" myself in that tight ball of twine. I saw it unwinding. I saw the me inside being born. The me that would get out of this place. The me that would live my life free, free of my walls, free of probation officers, and—most of all—free of my father. Every time I would feel the tightness in my chest, I would see that ball of twine unraveling and the me that was *really* me, escaping, becoming free. I had discovered the salvation of Phase One, and there would be no turning back.

*   *   *

I sat in my office across from Cheryl. She was an attractive woman in her mid-fifties with thick auburn hair. Her eyes, a dull green, stared at me, daring me to see past her controlled exterior.

Cheryl sat with her arms crossed tightly across her chest, hands clamped to the tightly crossed arms. Her legs were crossed as well, and her foot was swinging impatiently. Cheryl's body language clearly told me she had come to me well defended. If I was going to reach this woman at all, I would have to do it in the first five minutes, or she would shut down even more and I would lose my chance to reach her.

I closed my eyes, took a deep breath, and looked up and away. I took another breath and pictures about this woman began to form in my head. And as usually happens when I am working with someone, Spirit started speaking to me about her.

With that second breath I took, I could feel myself being flooded with love. It was literally pouring out of me and into this woman.

Slowly, I began to speak. "Cheryl, I can see how weary you are of taking care of other people. This has been your entire life's journey. From the time you were a little girl, you have been doing this. Taking care of Mommy, sister, everyone. As you became an adult it continued—in your relationships with men, and even in your career. It feels to me as if you have filled your life with so much of this caregiving that there is no time for you, correct?"

Only then did I look at Cheryl, who had tears running down her face as she nodded her head in acknowledgment.

I got up and walked over to where she was sitting. Kneeling down in front of her, I covered her hands with mine. Her tears continued to flow as I knelt in front of Cheryl, her hands in mine, while Spirit continued to pour love out of me and into her.

After a time she wiped her eyes, looked up, and said, "When my friend Judy told me about you, I thought she was exaggerating. I wasn't sure why I came here today. In fact, I almost canceled this session."

I laughed. "Yes, I had that feeling in meditation this morning."

"I'm glad I didn't cancel. I can't remember the last time I felt as much love as I feel right now. How do you do it?"

"I don't. Spirit comes through me to ignite that love within you. I call it the Divine Spark. You are a therapist, are you not?"

She looked at me incredulously and replied, "Did Judy tell you that?"

"No, she did not. Spirit did. Spirit also told me you are burned out. Too much energy going out, not enough coming back to you. It's time you learned to nurture yourself."

Cheryl smiled and nodded her head in agreement. As

we went on with the session, I took Cheryl through a phasing exercise similar to the one you've just done.

The hour went by quickly, as information and healing poured out of me. When the tape recorder clicked off, I knew, I felt it: Cheryl had heard the truth. She had been given tools and information to take with her. When Cheryl got up to leave, I reached out to hug her. She opened her arms, hugging me tightly. Her green eyes—once dull—were now shining; shining bright emerald-green. She had been touched at a deep level and would leave my office connected to that part of herself that was ready to love, and especially to love herself.

In a phone session with Cheryl a few months later, I could feel her excitement over the telephone. Intuitively, I could see her face beaming with love.

"Cheryl, how can I help you?"

"Actually, Dawnea, I wanted to share with you what's happened in my life over these last few months."

"Cheryl, you sound so different. Tell me all of the good stuff. What's up?"

She hesitated. "It's hard to put it all into words. . . . As I was driving away from your house back into town, I could clearly see all of the relationships in my life. I started taking mental inventory of all of the people I'd surrounded myself with. Most of them were takers. I determined from that moment on I would not say yes when I meant no, ever again."

"That's great, Cheryl."

"It gets better. I was to have lunch with a friend in

Santa Monica. We were barely seated and had just started looking at the menus when she burst into tears. Usually, I would panic over this. I would immediately begin to calm and nurture her out of it. Instead, I just sat there quietly listening to her ramble on and on about the same man who has been hurting her, lying to her, for the last five years. Twenty minutes went by without me saying a word. Finally—she noticed."

I smiled to myself as Cheryl was describing all of this, seeing the intuitive picture in my mind.

"So Christy looks up and says to me, 'What's wrong with you today, Cheryl?' "

" 'Oh, nothing,' I said.

"She shoots back at me, 'What do you mean, nothing? I've been telling you Michael has been seeing his neighbor, screwing her. I walked in on them.'

"I shrugged and said, 'So what else is new?'

"She stood up, her eyes blazing, and shouted, 'I don't have to take this. I don't know where our friendship has gone.'

"Dawnea, something inside of me got so calm. I lowered my voice and told her, 'I know where our relationship has gone, Christy. It never was there. It was only there when we were talking about your life, your problems. I am sick to death of hearing about Michael. He's a self-centered egomaniac. If you choose to continue to allow him to abuse you, well, that's your problem, I'd say.' "

I was smiling from ear to ear, knowing full well the inhibitions Cheryl had to have gotten over to say those words to her friend. "That must have taken a lot of courage, Cheryl."

"No, actually, it felt so good just to tell her the truth."

"What happened?"

Cheryl laughed. "She stormed out of the restaurant. I sat down, finished my lunch, went to Charles David, and bought a new pair of shoes."

"Right on, Cheryl. You spoke your truth and then went shopping. My kind of girl."

"Dawnea, since then I've been speaking my truth everywhere. I think you unleashed a monster."

"Nope, we unleashed your power. Isn't it cool?"

"Yes, yes, it is. . . . Oh, Dawnea, one more thing, I'm phasing with my clients. I've even come up with some of my own stuff. It's pretty powerful."

"Cheryl, I am so proud of you." Tears sprang to my eyes. The message was being carried from my office: one session with Cheryl and, in turn, to her people.

Right on!!!

Daniel sat in my office, staring restlessly out the window at the ocean below my home. His face was devoid of expression. His gray-brown eyes were blank. I looked away from him and took a deep breath, asking Spirit to open me so I could reach this troubled young man. As I breathed in my second or third breath, his pain hit me full force. I could literally see and feel the stored-up pockets of pain in his heart.

"Daniel, I feel so much pain locked inside of you. You

have been running from yourself for most of your life. Over the last year and a half things have really been intense for you. You have tried using drugs and alcohol to escape—but even that hasn't been working lately. You are lost, lost inside of the prison of pain you have stored inside you. I know your life has not been easy. I can see clearly the abuse that you were subjected to during your childhood."

Though I was not looking at Daniel, I could feel his body flinch at those words. I continued. "How sensitive you were. And how well you learned that sensitivity didn't work in your environment. You shut down. And you have been running ever since. In one way or another you have tried to hide your pain from yourself. You have pushed everyone away who tried to help you. You were afraid if you opened that door just a little, you would be hurt again. And now, today, you sit here and you do not want to live anymore. You are so tired of it all. Aren't you?"

I looked over at Daniel. His face was as white as the wicker chair his hands were clutching. Eyes wide with fear, he stared at me in disbelief. I saw his Adam's apple go up and down as he tried to swallow. I repeated the question: "Daniel, you're bone tired—tired of living, tired of trying—aren't you?"

Speechless, he nodded his head in agreement.

I didn't want to stop talking. I was afraid if I did, I would lose the rapport I had with him. "Daniel, I know how raw you are. I know this session was a gift to you from Molly. I know you have lost your job, lost your lover, and are about to get thrown out of your apartment. Listen to me, I have been where you are."

He looked around the room we were sitting in, out at the ocean below my home, then looked at me with a smirk on his face.

"Yes, I know what you see here today. And I thank Spirit every day of my life for these blessings. But there was a time in my life when I had driven myself to exactly the same place you are in now. I allowed myself to go deep into the darkest, most destructive part of myself until there was hardly anything left."

Daniel paused for a moment, then said, "It's hard to believe you would ever be in this place I'm in."

"I was—and what's worse, I didn't have someone to tell me that it would get better. But there was something inside of me that knew if I didn't get out of it, I would die. I also knew, if I took my own life, there would be consequences. I surrendered, Daniel, and in that surrendering I found something within myself that had long ago been buried."

"What was it?"

"Hope. And the knowledge I was not alone. I call it the Divine Spark. There is a way you can tap into it, right here, right now!"

He looked at me, doubt clouding his eyes.

"Let's try it. Close your eyes and take a deep breath in through your nose. Hold it. Hold it, blow it out through your mouth." I took Daniel through the circular breathing technique, then on to search his soul for those situations that needed to be healed by using Phase One.

"Now open your eyes and relax." I watched as I saw the pain leave Daniel's face. He opened his eyes. They were clear.

I smiled at him and said, "You see, it lives in you right this minute." With a twinkle in my eye I joked, "Don't even think of telling me you didn't feel that."

He laughed, and I continued. "Okay, I'm not going to sit here and tell you that, hallelujah! you are healed instantly. But I will tell you that if for just a second you can get out of your own way, if you will use what I've been sharing with you, you will find the way out of the dungeon you have created in your heart and in your mind. Then, and only then, will the shattered pieces of your life start to mend."

I turned and looked into Daniel's eyes. He looked back at me for a moment and said, "Dawnea, I believe you. I don't know why I believe you, but I feel something in this room. I feel something happening inside of me."

"Good, then go out there and face the mess you have made of your life. Know the Divine Spark is alive within you. You are not alone."

Six months went by, then one day I received a telephone call from Daniel telling me that since that day in my office, his whole life had changed. He'd listened and he was using the phasing technique every day. He even came up with a few of his own.

Daniel chose life, and he was willing to *use* what I taught him. (Get my point? If you don't use what you read in this book, it cannot help you.)

Daniel went to work on himself and the Divine Spark within him went to work right along with him.

He had a new job, a home, and he had met the love of his life. He told me he was out there sharing his experience with others. And by doing so he is igniting the Divine Spark in them!

Alison sat across from me, forehead furrowed in lines of stress. There were dark circles under her eyes. Obviously, she was working way too hard. She was very tense and could not sit still.

"Alison, as soon as I heard your voice, I knew this was a crisis session. Do you want me to pick your brain or do you just want to tell me what's up?"

She smiled ruefully. "I love it when I just let you go in there and pick my brain, but today I want to get down to it. I need some strong medicine, healer-woman." Alison laughed as she said those words.

"Okay, girlfriend, shoot."

"I'm putting this album together—the one you predicted I would get signed for two years ago. The band and I have been in the studio for the last seventy-two hours and I'm blocked. So fucking blocked, I can't get past it. They gave me creative control on this thing and I'm fucking it up. Everyone is looking at me, waiting to get on with the music, and I am stuck in this black hole. Shit, what am I going to do?" Tears started streaming down Alison's face.

I handed her a tissue and sat back in my chair, looking at her. Alison looked like her batteries were running low, to say the least.

"Okay, okay, Alison, let's go back to the point where you feel you started losing the flow."

"I don't know, Dawnea, it just left."

"No, I can see that is not the case. Something triggered you. What was it?"

She sat there, head in hands, rocking back and forth. I reached out to her with my heart and with my intuition. I "sent" her healing, soothing light; a soft blue surrounded by silver, gold, and white. It encompassed her whole body. I watched as the light swirled around and through her. Slowly she sat up, wiped her eyes.

I let out my breath. Through me, Divine Mind was reaching her.

"Hey, you zapped me, didn't you?"

I laughed. "Yeah, well, your batteries were running pretty low. Now back to my question."

"Slave driver."

"Uh-huh. Come on, Alison, quit stalling."

"Okay, three days ago, before I descended into hell, we were laying down tracks. One of the heads of the label came waltzing in with his little groupies in tow. He sat in the sound room listening for quite a while. I was watching him. I could just see by his vibe he was picking my music apart. I felt myself lose it, Dawnea. I just felt all of the magic of what I was doing drain away. He made me feel like shit."

"No, Alison, you made you feel like shit because you

bought into his trip. You know what you can do. You know how good you are. Did he say anything to you?"

"Yeah, yeah, he did. He came out of the sound room, raised his eyes, and said, 'In spite of that little-bad-girl act you've got going, you're good, Alison. That is—you're commercial. You're no Madonna, but you will sell this shit.'

"The fucker dropped that bomb and walked out. Can you believe it? Man, you could have cut the air with a knife after he left.

"My bass player came up and put his arm around me, saying, 'He's an asshole, Al, let's just get on with business.'" Alison's voice broke as she continued. "I couldn't go on after that, Dawnea. I was shattered."

I took a deep breath, then consoled her. "Honey, I am so sorry. I know how that must have hurt. Let me say this. No, you are not Madonna. There is only one Madonna. Just like there is only one Alison. And she is going to kick butt with this album."

Alison smiled sheepishly.

I offered a movie quote. "As Steve Martin says in *Leap of Faith,* 'The attack of the puny brains—been dealing with them all my life.'"

Alison burst out laughing. "D, you are too much!"

I barreled on. "The guy obviously wanted to make you feel insecure. Fuck him, Alison. You know what I told you. As I said today—and have said I don't know how many times over the last two years—this album is going to kick ass. You know that. He knocked you off your center. You and I are going to get you back there. I want you to pry your hands off that chair, close your eyes, take a deep breath, then let it go. . . ."

I took Alison through Phase One. I took her out of that ball of gnarled twine, the twine of her deepest fears, into the Divine Spark within her. . . . "Okay, Alison, when you are ready, open your eyes, be present, be in the now."

She opened her eyes, stretched out like a big cat, and smiled. "Thanks, D, I got my groove back."

Two days later Alison called me from the studio to thank me. She *had* gotten her groove back. (She also went on to "sell the shit" out of her first album.)

Cheryl, Daniel, and Alison faced different problems, but all three found help in Phase One, just as countless others I have worked with over the years have done. What we are looking for here is for you, like them, to return to your joy. To the part of you that knows what joy is, what freedom is, and what living a full life really is.

With Phase One nothing and no one will be able to keep you from your joy. All you've got to do is claim it. It's waiting for you. Just do it!

More important, that joy will stay with you. When things get rough out there in that big world, use Phase One. Go to your joy. The Divine Spark within you will not only break through your Conditioned Destiny, you'll have a good time doing it. You'll learn to laugh, and you will feel the love, the love within. Even in the face of life's challenges you will feel the love—the Divine's love for you.

Have you seen *Michael,* John Travolta's movie? See it. You will love it. Michael is an archangel. He's come back to earth. He's here for only a little while . . . and he plans to have one hell of a good time while he is here. Like Michael you can choose laughter, love, and joy—so what are you waiting for?

PHASE TWO

Help Is on the Way

> *"Master, at the most difficult times of
> my life, I saw only one set of footprints
> in the sand. Why was that?"*
>
> *The Master answered, "Because,
> my child, when you were so weary you
> couldn't walk, it was then I carried
> you."*

From the poem "Footprints"
Anonymous

At one time or another, in all of our lives, we have felt
as though no one hears our cries of anguish. We have all
experienced the lonely feeling that no one has the time
to listen to us pour out our frustrations and fears.

Even though we may have been taught that there is a
force "up there" with us—whether we call it God, Divine
Mind, the Master Jesus, the Goddess, Jehovah, or some
other name—at times like this we do not feel it. Instead,
we feel disconnected, alone.

In reality, we are never alone. Our souls know this—
even if our hearts and minds forget—that a Loving Presence is always there to gently touch our hearts, if we

will just allow ourselves to get out of our own way and feel that love.

Phase Two will help us out of our aloneness. It will reconnect us with someone or something greater by taking us back to the knowing within each of us that we are never alone. The place where it all began.

Choose the phasing technique that works best for you. After you've set the mood with the musical score you've chosen for this phase, sit comfortably erect and complete the circular breathing exercise you did in Phase One. Continue to take nice even breaths, remembering to breathe in through your nose and out through your mouth.

Now you can see the giant movie screen in your mind's eye. Focus on it for a moment. Right now it is completely blank; you are waiting for something to appear on the screen. You are waiting for the movie—your "mind movie"—to begin.

On the screen, larger than life, appears a beautiful white sand beach. It is sunset. As you look at the sky on the giant screen in your mind, it is alive with the pink, orange, and purple hues of the setting sun. I want you to connect your emotions with what you are seeing, so . . . let's use all of your senses. All of the senses that feed your emotions. Remember: intuition, imagination, and emotion. Connect them all. Make it real *now*!!

You can hear the gentle sound of the waves as they kiss the white sand. It's balmy; there is a slight tropical breeze blowing.

Now see yourself on the screen, on that white sandy beach. While you are watching yourself get into it, start to feel what you are seeing. Draw from the picture on the screen. Expound on the emotions that are coming up for you. Be fearless!!!

Feel the sand crunch underneath your bare feet. Feel the warm breeze blowing past your face. Smell the air; it is fragrant with the scent of flowers. Ah, yes, how alive you feel in this place! The pink, and now golden, sky is reflecting on the ocean, giving it a pearlescent glow. There is such a feeling of peace that you are one with the Universe in this beautiful place. Breathe in the breath of healing. See yourself standing in the gentle waves that are lapping on the sandy beach. Feel the warm water caressing your feet and ankles. On the screen in front of you, you close your eyes, allowing your emotions to respond. Allow yourself to feel, in this beautiful moment, the love that has been here all along. You no longer feel alone. You are a part of the nature that is surrounding you. (Don't even think about blocking the feelings that may be coming up right now, go with them.)

Allow the love to completely fill you. Breathe it in deeply. As you are absorbing the beauty of the sunset, absorb the love that is here for you.

On the giant screen in front of you, you open your eyes.

Your guide and teacher is standing right before you. I want you to look carefully at your guide. What do they look like? Take your time; don't be afraid. This is the first time you see your guide. I want you to see them in vivid detail. So much so, that they are as real as you are. Both of you: the you that is standing facing your guide on that giant screen and the you that is sitting there watching, feeling this encounter.

See them standing there on that giant screen in your mind, looking directly into your eyes. As you look into your guide's eyes, you can see their love and understanding for you. It registers on their face, on their entire being. Take that love into your heart and soul. They have been patiently waiting for you to acknowledge they are there.

Actually, your guide has traveled with you on your life's journey for a long time. Only now, after shutting off the clutter of thoughts from the day-to-day routine, only now that you have opened yourself up to the Divine's love for you, can you see and feel your guide and teacher.

Your guide gently takes your hand as you turn face-to-face. What are you feeling right now? Tell your guide how you feel about what is missing in your life. Pour out all of your pent-up feelings. If tears begin to fall, let them. If anger forms a choking ball in your throat, let it out. All of it. All of your disappointments, fears, and frustrations. Tell your guide everything. Then listen, listen with your thoughts and with your heart to your guide and teacher's response as you watch yourself and your guide in total communication on that giant screen in your mind.

If you want to, ask why it took your guide so long to reveal itself to you. Ask all the questions that have been lurking in the back of your mind—all the questions you would like to ask Infinite Mind. Your guide and teacher is a part of that Divine Source. When you're talking to your guide, you're connecting with your Divine Spark, so there's no need to rush through things. Take as long as you need to communicate with your guide. Once you have truly communed with each other, ask its name. Trust the first name that comes to you. It is correct. Now you have something your heart (your emotions) can identify with. Yeah!!

If you are having analytical second thoughts, pay them no mind. That's the voice of the good old Conditioned Destiny kicking in. *Get over it!* Stay in the moment. Your emotions are speaking truth. Do not allow your conditioned mind to get in the way!!!

From this moment on, every time you feel afraid, every time you feel alone, every time you are at a loss as to what to do, speak your guide's name. The answer will come.

Now let the screen in your mind disappear. I want you to keep in your heart all you have just experienced.

The *Star Wars* trilogy contains three of my favorite movies. I have watched them countless times. Each time I do, in those scenes where Luke Skywalker fights his inner and outer battles—and wins—my heart fills with joy as tears roll down my face. My daughter Heidi thinks I'm a little weird. Sometimes she finds me watching one of the trilogy, crying. She usually shakes her head and says, "Mom, how many times are you going to watch that movie? I can't believe they *still* make you cry!" I just nod as, eyes glued to the screen, I think about how *every* time I watch these films, they remind me that the capacity of the human spirit is amazing and that we can all fight hard to win our battles.

One of the scenes that is a guaranteed tearjerker for me is from the first movie, *Star Wars.* Luke Skywalker is boarding his fighter plane to destroy the massive Death Star. I often think of the biblical story of David and Goliath when I am watching this part. Luke is the squadron leader. He is up there fighting against the dark forces—determined to destroy the Death Star before those controlling it kill the people he loves, who are waiting and watching on another planet. One by one his fellow fighters are killed. He watches as the last one's plane is hit and plunges to its fiery death. As he turns around, you can see on his face the sadness of having lost yet another brave friend. Then he gathers his thoughts together and refocuses on the task at hand: to destroy the Death Star by firing his tiny missiles into the Death Star's heart. Suddenly you hear the gentle voice of his guide and teacher, Obi-Wan Kenobi, say, "Use the Force, Luke . . . let go." Luke stops, smiles wonderingly, knowing Obi-Wan, his beloved guide and teacher, is near. He turns back to his task, using his computer screen to focus on the target. Once again you hear Obi-Wan's gentle voice say to Luke, "Trust me."

He does. Luke shuts off his computer screen and uses the Force and Obi-Wan Kenobi's loving guidance to hit the target. Then you see the little missiles penetrating the Death Star and it shatters into a million pieces!

Like Luke you have your own guide and teacher. Listen to the voice that is speaking to you. And trust the voice of your guide.

May the Force be with you!!!

I have so many memories of times in my life when a guide, a teacher, a loving presence, came to me. This one is especially dear. Every time I think back on this experience, my eyes fill with tears.

I was about twelve years old. Early one morning,

while it was still dark outside, I was awakened by a bright light at the foot of my bed. At first, I wasn't sure if I was still sleeping or if I was awake. I sat up and looked at the light. I could see a man's figure outlined in the brightness. With a croaking voice I asked, "Who are you?"

He stretched out his hand and said, "I will make you fishers of men."

I had heard this scripture many times over in my childhood. The Master Jesus said it to his disciples. I squeezed my eyes tightly shut. Stubbornly, I shook my head no. No way would I walk that path; no way would I end up like my father.

I could still feel the bright light on my face. I did not want to open my eyes. Then I felt a hand gently touch me. And my heart filled with such love. Never in my life had I experienced that much or that kind of love. Tears ran down my face.

I saw myself as the little girl I was then, holding the hand of the Master Jesus. We were standing on a ramp suspended in the air; there were thousands of people under us. As I was throwing rose petals to the people, their hands were reaching frantically to grab the flowers. I looked up at the Master Jesus, my eyes filled with questions.

Then the picture changed. I wasn't a little girl anymore. I was a grown woman. The Master Jesus and I were standing on that same ramp suspended above the crowd. Only, this time, I was talking into a microphone. The Master Jesus was standing next to me, smiling.

When the vision faded, I was sitting straight up in my bed. My entire bedroom *smelled* like roses.

Many years later, shortly after I'd started serving people professionally, I was meditating in my office one morning. During my meditation the same vision came to me. Tears readily came as I remembered that frightened twelve-year-old. That love, that beautiful, radiant love, filled me once again. And like so many years before, the entire room smelled of roses.

There have been many times over the years, when I am in a difficult session with someone who has suffered greatly, that I ask for a certain kind of help. The kind that beams unconditional love out to that suffering person who's with me. When that help arrives, I will feel that presence—His presence—in the room, and I will smell roses—every time. Am I the only one who smells it? No.

I must tell you a funny story. One of my dear friends is a Capricorn—one of the more skeptical signs of the Zodiac. In spite of her skepticism in some areas, she is a wonderful body worker. One Saturday she came to my home to work on me. There was no one in the house except for the two of us. We were in the treatment room with the door closed.

This was at a time when I was extremely burned out. As Judy was working on me, I could hear footsteps in the hall. Seconds later a gentle rose-scented breeze brushed my face. Tears rolled down my cheeks; I knew He was in the room helping her to heal me.

We finished, and she went out to wash her hands. I

heard her call my daughter Heidi's name. I knew Heidi wasn't home; she was on a shoot. I also knew whose footsteps she had heard.

When I came out of the treatment room, I saw Judy sitting in my big chair in the living room, her long legs drawn up around her, eyes as big as saucers. "Whose footsteps were those, D? They sure as hell weren't Heidi's."

I laughed and told her, "No, they weren't Heidi's."

"And that smell in the treatment room. That wasn't incense."

I giggled, saying, "Right again."

"I heard footsteps and I smelled roses," Judy insisted. Judy had known me for years; she'd heard more than a lot about my life, my past, my work. Her eyes got wider as she stated, "Oh, my God! It was Him, wasn't it?"

I nodded my head in agreement.

Wonder filled her face.

I was sitting, looking out at the ocean, waiting for Karen. She had called me for a telephone session. She wanted to speak to me about the in-office session we had done two weeks before, when I had taken her on a journey that led her to her spiritual teacher.

"Dawnea, I must tell you that since our last session, I have been feeling so much different."

"How so, Karen?"

"Well, when I was in your office and you took me on the journey to meet my guide, I wasn't sure if it was because I was with you, in your environment, that I connected with him, or if I just made the whole thing up. I wanted to believe he was with me, but I just wasn't sure. So for about a week I was afraid to go back and listen to the tape of the session, and I was afraid to say his name. I even wrote about my fear in my journal, but I just wasn't sure."

"Right on, Karen, the journaling really helps you to open up," I told her.

With an excited voice she went on. "Well, maybe that's why this happened. A couple of days ago I visited friends up north. I took a long walk, hiked up this hill that looked out over the ocean. I closed my eyes and breathed like you taught me. Then I felt something brush my arm. It gave me the chills."

I began to get a visual picture of Karen standing on the hillside.

"In my mind he was there, Dawnea—bigger than life—on the screen in my mind. But—and now it gets really weird—I kept hearing someone say, 'Open your eyes.' I didn't want to, I wanted to keep my focus on the screen. But someone just kept repeating the words 'Open your eyes.' Finally I did, and you know what? I saw him!!! I swear I saw him standing right next to me."

Karen paused, then continued, her voice filled with awe and with tears. "He is so beautiful. He's Indian. A tall, handsome brave with long hair. It was just a second, then he vanished, but I know he is real. I know I saw him standing with me on that hill. Dawnea, is this weird?"

"No, not at all. I've had the same experience many times. The first time it happens, it's a little unnerving, to say the least."

"You know what, Dawnea? I feel him near me all the time now. Not just when I call his name, or write about him in my journal, but all of the time. For the first time in my life I sense I'm not alone."

"How does that feel, Karen?"

"Like I'm walking hand-in-hand with Spirit."

I smiled to myself, deeply touched by this young woman's courage. "That's exactly what you are doing," I told her.

Ray was sitting in my office, eyes darting back and forth. I had been working with Ray for over five years and had never seen him this agitated. Ray is a tall man, with a well-defined, muscular body. His presence intimidates most people—especially when he pulls up on his Harley-Davidson motorcycle. We had talked about his ability to intimidate people in many previous sessions. He always smiles and admits his ego loves all that attention. Out of the many people I have counseled, I would say Ray is one of the more skeptical when it comes to "woo-woo" matters. Anything he can't see or touch isn't real to him, "except God and Jesus Christ, of course," he claims.

Ray came to me mostly for business advice. But once in a great while he would let me go off on a tangent on spiritual subjects. This particular day he was different.

I took a deep breath as I looked out the window. "So, Ray," I began, "what's up? You are definitely not yourself today."

"I had something happen to me I can't explain. It scared the hell out of me."

I looked over at Ray and decided not to "hook in" yet. I wanted to hear him out before I went into my telepathic space.

"Go ahead, tell me what happened."

In spite of his agitation his ego was still intact. He smiled his sly smile and mocked, "Can't you 'pick up' on it, Dawnea?"

I shot him a look. "Cut the bullshit, Ray, just tell me what happened."

He took a deep breath and told his story. "I was driving over Kanan Road. It was around midnight. All of a sudden, out of nowhere, I heard this cry . . . like something was hurt. I kept driving, thinking it was my imagination, but I heard it again. Mind you, I had all of the windows rolled up and I had my CD player on. Something inside of me made me stop the car. I pulled over to the side of the road and rolled down my window. Something told me to get out of the car.

"I thought I was losing it. I got out of the car and started walking. In the brush I found this little baby coyote. Its head was split open, blood pouring everywhere, but it was still hanging on. I picked the little guy up and carried him to my car. I used my car phone to call the nearest emergency vet. Fortunately, there was one very close to where I found him. I wrapped him in my leather jacket and rushed him into the emergency room."

I watched Ray as he told me his story. He no longer looked like the arrogant man who felt he had to impress people. He looked very much like a vulnerable little boy. I listened quietly as he continued.

"I don't know, Dawnea, it was weird. It was like I felt I had to save this animal. I felt in doing so, I would save a part of myself." Under his breath he whispered, "A part no one ever cared about."

"Were they able to save the little guy?"

Tears filled his eyes as he shook his head no.

I wanted to reach out to Ray, I wanted to go over to where he was sitting and hug him, but I knew that would be hard for him to accept, so I reached out with my heart and with Spirit's love for him.

He caught himself, saying, "But this is not all of it. This is where it gets a little confusing, more than a little strange. I was driving over Kanan the very next night. All of a sudden in front of my headlights was a baby coyote. I slammed on my brakes and stopped just short of where he was, then he vanished. Just vanished—right in front of my eyes. At first I thought he ran away, but I knew he didn't. And now it's very strange. I *feel* him with me all the time. You know me, Dawnea, I don't believe in this kind of stuff."

"Ray, for centuries American Indians have believed that animals can be our spirit guides. Looks like you've made yourself a friend."

Ray looked at me—not with the usual skepticism in his eyes, but rather with relief.

"Yep," he said, "that's what I thought."

The following two years of Ray's life were rather turbulent. Let's say that Spirit gave him some hard lessons in humility. I saw him through that time, and I am happy to say, he is on the other side of it—a much wiser, a much humbler man. More often than not, whenever we spoke, he would mention his little buddy: the coyote watching out for him.

Amanda looked up at me with tearstained eyes. Two weeks earlier she had lost her brother, Donnie, in a violent car accident. The ravages of grief were etched all over her beautiful face.

I didn't speak to her for several minutes. We sat in silence as she was filled with the Divine's love. I could feel it pouring through me to her. Several more minutes passed, then Amanda took a tissue from the box at her feet, wiped her nose, and in a voice barely above a whisper, she spoke: "Dawnea, why did this happen to him? He was so young and he loved everyone." Her voice broke as she fought to continue speaking. "He was such a good soul, why did God have to take him? We all loved him so."

Gently, I tried to answer her anguished questions. "Amanda, God doesn't take people from us. Each one of us chooses when we come here to earth and when we leave. I feel that Donnie had greater work to do from the other side."

She looked up at me, anger filling her eyes, as I continued.

"I know. It sounds like a trite answer, but you have my word. This is my intuition speaking. If I had a different message, I would tell you. You've been working with me for eight years now, you know I never sugarcoat anything. I'm not about to start now."

"I know, I know," she said. "I'm just so angry at his loss. And I feel so alone. He and I were closer than brother and sister. He was my best friend. What am I going to do?" As her body shook with sobs, I sat beside her and I held her gently, rocking her.

"Honey, I know how much this hurts, I can feel your anguish. Just let it all go. Here—now—in my office, tell God how you feel. Shout it if you have to. Tell Donnie how you feel, just let it all out."

Amanda did, and I let her. I just sat there and held her and let her cry it all out. When she was totally quiet, I sat back in my chair and asked, "Amanda, how are you feeling?"

"Pretty drained."

"Amanda, are you up for doing some phasing with me?"

We'd done some phasing work in the past, and I was getting the message loud and clear that it was time to do some more.

"Honey, I know you're drained, but will you trust

me? Spirit is prompting me to do this work with you right now."

She looked up at me. She could see by the expression on my face that I felt compelled to phase with her. She took in several deep breaths, held each one, then blew it out. "All right, Dawnea, I'm ready."

I took Amanda on a phasing journey. We went to the sandy beach. As the guide began to walk toward her I could "see" it was Donnie. We finished the phase and I brought her back to the room we were in when we started our journey. I could feel Donnie's presence in the room. In fact, I could see him standing next to Amanda.

She opened her eyes and asked, "He's here, isn't he, Dawnea? Donnie is here with me."

"Yes, yes, he is, Amanda."

She started to cry once again. Then she told me, "Dawnea, when we went to the white sand beach, he was waiting for me there. He told me he'd always be with me. He said we were soul mates. Said that he was assigned to me, to be my teacher, my guide. He also told me that I'd better not chicken out. He told me I'd better go to France to pursue my modeling career. He laughed and said he'd always wanted to go to Paris, now he could. My God, did I make all this up?"

I shook my head no and told her she hadn't. I told her that when we were phasing together, I could see Donnie on the white sand beach with her.

I laughed lightly and added, "However, I did not eavesdrop."

"Dawnea, thank you for this. You don't know how much this means to me."

"It's okay, Amanda, that's what I'm here for."

Each one of these people you've just read about had a different experience with their guide/teacher. The point is, they all allowed themselves to be touched by that something or someone greater than their old conditioning.

Granted, in Amanda's case it took a crisis to get her there, but Donnie is there for her now.

Your own guide and teacher is waiting for you. How cool is that?

I want you to know that you can trust whatever or whoever comes to you in this phase. Search your soul and trust your intuition; it does not lie.

Isn't it a relief to know you are not alone? From this moment on, for the rest of your life, you know there is always that special guide no farther away than a thought. Whatever dilemma you are facing, turn within, use your phasing, and call on your guide. The answer will be there. Do not even think about not trusting it!!!

Preproduction II

When you're very young, you don't have the ability to reason out certain things. You are totally at the mercy of your environment and the people in it. That's how you survive, with the simple courage of childhood—the same courage that still lives in the innocent child buried inside of you years later.

Yes, you do survive, but you don't always escape. Deep inside you carry around those people who hurt you, with words, with actions, even with the slightest disapproving glance. The sense of alienation brought about by these wounds may be buried, but it is not dead—it lives on. All the success in the world will not change that. That part of you—to this day—lives and breathes within you.

The bizarre thing I've observed over the years is that a horrific environment is very often a breeding ground for phenomenal creative energy. What you did back then (when you couldn't handle the world you lived in) was create a world inside you where no one could hurt you. Think how amazing the mind is. *Your* mind. No wonder most of the creative people I know come from environments that forced them to shut off emotionally—starting the creative process that continues to thrive.

Let's go back to your past. You can control those voices inside you. You know, the ones that speak to you right when you're in the middle of an important meeting, or out on a date, or with a friend. The voices that say, *If they only knew who you really are.* The ones that cause icy traces of fear to run up your spine.

Let's talk about the voices for a moment. First things first: Surf that soul of yours and identify who they are. By doing this you are commanding power over them. You are in control of your mind, of your life.

Now we need your subconscious and your emotions to get the message. How do you get your subconscious to respond to you? You bring these suckers to the surface, give them faces and give them names. Like: Mom, Dad, teacher, whatever, whoever. You take power over yourself.

Before we take this phasing journey, I want you to do some "prep" work: single out each person from your past who has hurt you. Start from the top: the person who stands out in your mind and heart as having left the most scars on your heart. From there I want you to make a list of everyone in your life, for as far back as you can remember, who caused you pain. Every person who told you that you couldn't have it, couldn't be it, or couldn't do it. For some of you it's even worse. Write down the names of those who physically and emotionally abused you, so much so that you gave up hope or you were afraid to try anything.

This will be no easy task; those wounds run deep. But they must be addressed in order for you to heal. I know it's hard, but just start and the rest will follow. The names will come and the memories with them will come as well. Don't be afraid. Whatever it was, you survived it. You're here. Now we want more than just survival; we want you to start living, really living, your life!

Start with your childhood. (Even before, if you believe in reincarnation.) Let that mind of yours run free. I mean everyone; I'm not saying these people *meant* to hurt you, or to make you feel isolated, but that's the message that got stored in your soul—and is still there today. Now we want to change that data. It's not so easy to do. It's not as though I can say, "Oh, here's a magic wand . . . *zap,* you're healed!"

I know this is hard. You can do it! I know you can. You wouldn't have found your way to this book if you weren't ready.

If you stay with it, it will work. You will know because you will feel the difference by the way you react in the outside world.

Old patterns die hard. So when they flare up, and they will, you will know who is speaking to you. And you will deal with it, whether you are in the middle of a meeting, or the middle of the night.

The real secret to this is quite simple: You have to want to be out of the drama bad enough to let it go. I have seen a lot of people who love the drama. If that's the case, they're going to stay stuck in their shit. Because that shit gets them a lot of mileage, a lot of attention. It's your choice. What do you say?

Let's go to work.

Put on some music. (I think Led Zeppelin might work here.)

Take a large piece of paper; I like to use those big yellow legal pads for this. Have your favorite pen or pencil handy. You may be doing a lot of writing here, so use something cool to write with.

Sit down in a comfortable chair at a table or a desk.

Place the pad or paper in front of you with your pen or pencil on top of it.

Close your eyes, take a deep breath, start your circular breathing. Take three deep breaths in and out, open your eyes, and pick up your pen or pencil.

Draw a line down the center of the paper.

When the first name pops into your head, write it down. Directly across from that name, write down the *first* emotion you feel. (Trust what comes to you. This is *not* the time to edit.)

Let your mind and your emotions merge. Take all the time you need. Use all the paper you need. Shout it out as you write it down, if it helps. The important point is to get it out of you and onto that paper.

After you've exhausted yourself getting it all out on paper, take that paper and burn it. That's right, have a ceremonial burning of all that stored-up pain. Do a little victory dance while the pain of your past is turning to ashes. Then take those ashes and scatter them somewhere in nature. Give them back to Mother Earth. She will help in your healing.

Yeah!!! We're ready to roll!!!

Turning Back the Hands of Time

Walk up to it
Walk over it
Find the courage to
Burn that bridge, burn the bridge
Burn that bridge, burn the bridge
Burn the way back to the pain
Light is just beyond the ridge
And burn that bridge

From the song "Burn that Bridge"
Words by Molly Pasutti

Phase Three is a powerful journey to the place inside you where deep pockets of pain are stored. Through Phase Three you will feel yourself breaking free of those painful memories.

Phase Three will take you "back in time" to the exact moment that pain began; to the circumstances and the people who were there and cocked the emotional triggers in you.

Through phasing you will face that moment and all that was there, and in doing so you will move beyond it. Beyond it to a place of freedom, a place of love.

*   *   *

Set the scene, create the mood, sit comfortably, and begin your circular breathing. Feel yourself letting go of the world "out there"—just like you do when you are sitting in a dark theater, waiting for the movie to begin. Block out everything around you, except for your breathing. When you reach the seventh breath, call up the giant screen in your mind. Feel the nervous anticipation building inside you. You are waiting for the movie—your movie—to begin.

Search your soul to find a place from your past that holds deep emotional memories of something that happened to you. An event so degrading, so painful, that it was there, in that moment, that you shut down your emotions. You shut them down to survive.

Let the scene of that memory appear on the screen in your mind. Just go with the first thing that appears. You might be seeing a house you lived in as a child, or a classroom where you were once a student. Maybe it was on a vacation, or visiting relatives, or just being totally alone. Whatever the scene is, on the giant screen in your mind, trust it! It may start to fade as old emotions surface. That is your past conditioning. It thinks it needs to protect you from that long-ago time. It thinks it needs to keep it secret. Do not allow that to happen. You're already protected—your Divine Spark is with you. Trust the process and stay with it!

Let the reel in your mind advance. Place yourself as you were in that moment on the screen in front of you. Reexperience what happened at that time, in that place. Allow yourself to feel the emotions. Whatever is happening up there on the screen and inside of you, remember this: You survived it; you are here, bravely facing it.

The picture on the screen in your mind, and the emotions that are connected to this picture—the emotions you buried long ago—are the keys to reconnecting you to your Divine Spark. It feels as if live emotional wires inside of you that were once running everywhere and nowhere are now reconnecting. Yes, I know it is painful, but it is a critical point in your phasing. Go with it!!

As the Bible says, "And ye shall know the truth and the truth shall set you free." Allow yourself to see and feel this truth. The picture on the giant screen in your mind is real. Even though your conditioning might be kicking in right now, trying to fight this truth, emotions do not lie! Let it all come for you; acknowledge every little part of it. Let the emotions intensify. You can now give yourself permission to experience all that you were forced to hold inside. So, let it rip!!! See the other characters in the movie. Who are the bad guys or girls? Let yourself see the whole picture, know the whole script. Take as long as you need to get it out in the open. You will know when you're ready for the next step of phasing: You start breathing evenly. It is time to move on.

What do you want to do right now? You're not going to run and hide anymore. You're going to do something for that person up there.

So, on the giant screen, see the you that is sitting there watching and feeling join the you whose innocence and self-worth are being stripped away. Just like that! You're up there together. It's real because you see it, you feel it—and you made it happen.

Fearlessly, you see the "you of today" standing in between the helpless "you of the past" and the bad guys or girls who are trying to destroy the hopes and dreams of that "helpless" you.

Using the stored-up emotions you have right now, command them to get the hell away. Tell them they have no right to treat anyone the way they have been treating this defenseless person (the you of the past). Just as the good guys show up in the movies at the last minute to rescue the person in danger, right now you are rescuing yourself. You are fighting the battle that has raged inside of you all these years. And you are winning.

Take as long as you need to absorb all that has just transpired. You have finally won. You are free.

Take a deep breath of freedom. Let yourself resume even breathing, and allow the screen in your mind to fade away. Stay with the sweet taste of victory. You've earned it!!!

In *The Prince of Tides,* at the very beginning, you hear Nick Nolte's southern-accented voice drawl as he speaks these words: "I don't know when my parents began their war against each other. But I do know, the only prisoners they took were their children.

"When my brother, sister, and I needed to escape, we developed a ritual. We found a silent, soothing world where there was no pain. A world without mothers or fathers. We would make a circle bound by flesh and blood and water, and only when we felt our lungs betray us would we rise toward the light and the fear of what lay in wait for us above the surface.

"All of this was a long time ago, before I chose not to have a memory."

The camera shows those three children running down a ramp, jumping into the water. Joining hands, they float beneath the water. In that moment they are safe from a world filled with pain. You watch Nick take his journey up there on that giant screen, remembering and reliving his troubled past. In doing so he heals himself and his sister as well.

We (my father, stepmother, half brothers, and half sisters) lived in a house on Java Street in Inglewood, California. I must have been about six or seven years old at the time.

After dinner my father would go into his room to "study and pray."

My stepmother would put a wooden chair in the middle of the kitchen. She'd look at me and say, "Devil, you are a liar." She'd grab me by the hair, bend me over that wooden chair, take the steel end of a fly swatter, and proceed to beat me while saying, "I cast that demon Satan out. In the name of Jesus, I cast him out."

You know how I got through those nights, those beatings? I would sing the song "Somewhere Over the Rainbow." I would sing the words to that song over and over in my mind while she was beating on me. I would see that giant movie screen where I first saw *The Wizard of Oz.* I would see myself in the land of Oz. I was Dorothy. I was standing in the place where all the little Munchkin people were dancing around. In my mind I was far away from Java Street, far away from my stepmother, and far, far away from the welts that were stinging my legs.

"Who wants to share?" I asked the circle of five sitting with me on the floor. This was the third Intraphase workshop I had taught, and we had just broken into small groups after a group phasing exercise. The circle I was working with sat quietly, each one lost in his or her own memories of the phasing we had just completed.

I was surprised when the shiest member of the circle started speaking. Cary kept his eyes fixed on the patterns he was making with his finger in the carpet. In a voice just above a whisper he began, "You know, Dawnea, I had a hard time at first. My old conditioning just didn't want to let go. But I want these changes so badly, I willed myself to concentrate on your voice and the screen in my mind. At first I felt something the size of a boulder was stuck in my throat."

Susan, a young woman in her twenties with almond-shaped eyes, shook her head. "You felt that too?"

Cary smiled and continued. "I was back home. I was twelve years old. My brother was taunting me. 'You'll never have anything. You'll never be anything. You are a slug. A pimple on the butt of humanity.'

"My brother, Don, was a manic-depressive. Everything and everyone in our family revolved around him and his mood swings. God, could he be evil! If I retaliated at all, I would be the one punished. In that moment, watching the scene on my 'mind screen,' all of my pent-up anger from the past flooded inside of me. At first it was scary. I thought I was going to jump up and start screaming, 'Go to hell, you selfish bastard,' but I took a deep breath, letting the feelings flow. The anger was definitely there, but there was also something else. It was like a light went on inside of me. I began to realize: This is why I am so defensive, this is why I can't keep a job. This is definitely why I am afraid to love. I am afraid if I let anyone near me, I will abuse them with my anger."

Cary shook his head. It was clear to me the realizations were hitting him—and hitting him hard.

"I think we all should congratulate Cary. It takes a lot of courage to relive an experience like yours, Cary, and it takes even more courage to acknowledge part of that experience."

One by one the circle reached out to Cary. I fought back the tears as I watched yet another breakthrough.

A few weeks later Cary called me for a private session. In that session we talked about his breakthrough in the Intraphase workshop. He shared with me how dramatically his feelings had shifted. He had moved out of the anger and seen his brother as a victim—of his own stored-up anger and rage. Cary had then shared with his brother his realizations about him.

"Dawnea, I forgave him. It felt so good to be able to let it go. I mean, really let it go."

"How did your brother respond?"

"The usual. He is in denial. I realized he *likes* being the victim. It's gotten him a lot of mileage."

"Yes, Cary, there are many people like that."

"Well, I'm not one of them. I'm going to go out there and manifest the life I deserve."

As well Cary did. Within a year he had met his soul mate, Anna. That was back in 1988. He now has three beautiful children. I speak to him from time to time. He is still "phasing." He is still working on his life.

That's what it takes. It is the belief in yourself today that creates the miracles of tomorrow.

Suzette's steps were almost silent as she walked out of the treatment room into my office and sat in the chair across from me. Her tear-stained face was cast downward. She could not look at me.

"Suzette, don't feel strange about not wanting to look at me. When I take someone that far into herself, the intimacy is almost too much."

I laughed, trying to break the tension, as I continued. "Don't feel bad. You are not the first person who came out of my treatment room afraid to look me in the face. Poor baby. You were so frightened. Scared to death of what your mind was showing you. And your emotions were heaving so much that your body began responding to those locked-up emotions, those locked-up memories."

Suzette looked up at me. "Is that why I rolled myself up in a ball?"

I nodded, answering, "Yes, you automatically put yourself in the fetal position. The survival position."

Suzette started to cry, the tears flowing down her high cheekbones. "Dawnea, I wanted to do this with you so badly. You know I flew out from Dallas just so I could do this session. But I had no idea it would be that real . . . that painful. Oh, my God, no wonder I can't trust men."

I had just taken Suzette through a regression session. Regression is like phasing, only more intense. The main difference is that I am in the room, guiding the person to the most difficult memory of his or her past, and allowing Spirit to come through my hands, my thoughts, and my heart to heal the person I am working with.

Let me say right here that while you can't do regression work alone, you don't need me in the room to phase. With your own courage connected to the Divine Spark, you can experience the same intense breakthrough Suzette did. You just have to want it bad enough and be ready to let it go.

Suzette is a beautiful girl in her early twenties. She is a singer and model. When she first came to see me I knew intuitively that there was something radically blocking her. After a few sessions, in-office and on the phone, when I knew I could not break through to her any other way, I suggested regression work. (Regression work is the last tool I will use with someone. It is not for everyone. It is extremely confronting work.) It took Suzette a year to gather the courage to come to me for the session. Looking at her sitting there (knowing what she had just experienced), I was so proud of her.

"Suzette, do you want to talk about what just happened in there?"

"Yes and no. Part of me is already telling myself I made it up."

"Nope, you definitely did not make it up. Your body does not lie. Look at how you responded to what you saw happen to you in my treatment room."

"Yes, Dawnea, before today, every time I thought of my bedroom in that house on Winston Street, I would get physically ill. And weirder, every time I see the color green I get anxiety attacks."

"Ah, green was the color of your bedroom door, was it not?"

Suzette nodded.

"Suzette, after a session like this, it helps to talk about it; it reinforces the truth. Do you feel okay with that?"

She sighed. "Yes, I felt you there with me, Dawnea. I felt you in that room when he came in. I was terrified, but I also knew I would be okay. Does that make sense?"

I nodded my head as I looked into Suzette's eyes, remembering what I had just gone through with her. From the time she was five years old until the age of eleven, whenever her uncle visited her home to "baby-sit" (so her parents could go out drinking), he would come into her room and sexually abuse her. In my treatment room Suzette relived those experiences. She faced all of the degradation, all the shame, that took place every time that man put his hands on her. She watched and experienced his threats about what he would do the next time, if she told anyone. She lived with those secrets locked inside of her until—with her courage and the help of the gifts Spirit has blessed me with—she remembered. She allowed herself to experience all of the memories of that horrible time. All of the shame, all of the fear, and all of the anger and rage. The rage of being a child, helpless against the sick mind of an adult.

"Dawnea, after I saw what he did, I went into this place where that little girl he was abusing was my beautiful little daughter. My skin crawled. Then I was pissed. How dare he?

"Remember when you told me to throw open the door to my room, walk in, and face him?"

Looking at this brave young woman, I confirmed, "Yes, that was the turning point."

Her eyes glistened with tears as she spoke. "Yes, it was. I saw myself go in that room and walk up to him. His back was to me and he had his pants down. His bare butt was hanging out. At the same time I could see what he was doing to that little girl, my little girl . . . me.

"I clawed his naked butt with my nails, and he turned around. When he saw it was an adult and he'd been caught, he hid his face. Can you believe it? The chickenshit bastard."

I saw the same thing Suzette had seen in the treatment room.

"Suzette, I saw what you did next. You pulled his hands down and spit right in his face. You looked him in the eye and said, 'You aren't worth the dirt I spit on, old man.' "

She looked at me and asked, "You were there with me, weren't you, Dawnea?"

I nodded.

Suzette's eyes narrowed as she continued. "There was something else. As I looked at him, he looked shrunken and pathetic. All the anger went away. I felt something locked deep inside of me break free. God, it felt good."

"Good for you, Suzette, but there was something else. What did you do for that little cowering girl—that half-naked little girl who was huddled in the corner of her bed?"

Tears sprang to her eyes as she murmured, "I took her in my arms; I took her out of that house. I bought her a new dress and I took her to the state fair. When we were riding on the Ferris wheel above the city, I promised her I would never let anyone hurt her, not ever again."

"And so, Suzette, that means you can never allow anyone to hurt you, ever again."

I opened the door to my office to see a gorgeous hunk of young man sitting on my white sofa. He turned, looking at me with the most beautiful green eyes I had ever seen. While his eyes were luminescent green, they were also filled with pain. He stood, towering over me. He was wearing tight-fitting jeans and a black T-shirt. He smiled, showing perfectly white teeth. He extended his well-shaped hand, wide with long fingers. (I have a thing about hands, so I always notice them.)

Sam was picture perfect. He was an actor, not only gorgeous but talented as well. But there was such an emptiness, such a void, I couldn't wait to get to work.

As we sat down in my office, Sam immediately began drumming his manicured nails on the arm of the chair. I thought to myself, *Yep, he's well defended. I've got my work cut out for me.*

"Sam, if you are willing, I'd like to do some phasing with you today. I think you'll benefit from that experience far more than a counseling session. Are you up for it?"

He shifted uneasily in his chair and looked at me, puzzlement in his eyes. "Dawnea, Joey told me about soul surfing and phasing, but I thought you were going to tell me about myself, about my life."

I hesitated, trying to find the right words to put him at ease. "I could do that, yes. However, earlier this morning in meditation, I received some very clear instructions. I have to trust what Spirit is instructing me to do. I need you to trust me on this. Tell you what . . . let's try it. If you aren't satisfied, I'll start talking. Deal?"

Skepticism etched his face. "Okay . . . if that's the best way to it," he reluctantly agreed.

"Great! Let's get started. Sit up straight, feet on the floor, hands resting on knees, palms upward. Now take a deep breath through your nose . . . hold it . . . let it out through your mouth."

Whenever I am working with someone, be it intuitive counseling or a phasing session, I have a musical score playing in the background. I watched as Sam relaxed into the music and then into himself. I took a deep breath, then started Sam on his journey. "Sam, in front of you, see a giant screen. Like a movie screen. Can you see it?"

In a soft voice he answered, "Yes, yes, I can."

"Good. Now . . . on that screen I want you to see yourself at age fourteen."

I watched his body jerk at those words. "It's all right, Sam, you can do this."

I waited a few moments. "Do you see yourself at fourteen?"

He croaked, "Yeah, yeah, I see that fat little kid that I was."

My heart reached out as I heard the anger and rage in Sam's answer.

Gently I coaxed, "Sam, tell me about that little kid. What are you seeing on the screen? What are you feeling inside?"

Several moments went by. I could feel Sam fighting with himself.

"Sam, where are you?"

"I'm in fourth-period gym class."

"What's going on?"

"We are about to go out and run the track."

I glanced at Sam. His upper lip was glistening with beads of perspiration. He was wringing his damp hands together. He had crossed his legs. I knew this was not easy for him.

Gently, I again coaxed him on. "Sam, it's okay, you're doing just fine. Let's go on. What's happening up there on that screen in your mind?"

He sighed a heavy sigh and said, "We're going to run the track like we do every day. Only, I can't keep up, I'm too fat. God, this is humiliating. Do I have to go on?"

"Yes, you do, Sam."

His voice now sounded like that frightened young man I could intuitively see him describing. "The other smart-ass jocks are running by me, slapping me on the ass, saying, 'Come on, fat boy, you don't want Coach Johnson to kick your ass again today, do you?' Just then the coach comes up beside me and gets in my face. 'Come on, you little fucker, I'm going to teach your fat ass to run if it kills you. Little momma's boy. You better get those fat globs you call legs moving.'"

When I looked at Sam, I saw tears rolling down his face.

Several moments of silence followed. I let Sam be. I was allowing him to bring up this devastating memory.

His voice—a voice of rage—finally spoke: "Coach kept poking at me, egging me on. My heart was pounding so hard, my whole body was screaming in pain. I tripped over my own feet, fell in the dirt, and I just lay there. . . . I wanted to die."

"Where is the coach, Sam?"

He laughed this wounded laugh, then answered,

"He's kicking me. All the boys are standing around me now; he's kicking me, calling me a fat, stupid fuck."

"Sam, right now, I want you to suspend that picture on the screen. Take a deep breath and let it go. My God, you are brave. Now I want you—the man who's sitting here today—to join that poor young boy lying on the ground. I want you to tell that coach what you think of him. I want you to demand he stop kicking and demeaning that helpless fourteen-year-old. Do it, Sam. Do it now!"

Sam's rage cut loose. "You ignorant asshole. Who do you think you are?"

"Sam, what are you doing? What's going on up there on that screen?"

He laughingly said, "Tell you the truth, the coach is not so big after all. I've got him by his sweatshirt and I'm twirling him around in a circle. He falls to the ground. Funny, I don't need to do anything. I just look at him and say, 'You're pathetic.'

"I walk over to my fourteen-year-old, pick him up, and say, 'Come on, buddy, let's get the hell out of here.' I turn and never look back. Man, that feels good."

"Good work, Sam. Let the screen disappear. Come back to this room. Take a deep breath, open your eyes."

He opened his beautiful green eyes, no longer empty, but filled with warmth.

"Whew! That was intense. You know why I came here today?"

I knew, but I wanted him to tell me. "Why?"

"Because you know my last few films have done real

well. I'm on my way, or so my agent tells me. But the more I get, the more I do, the worse I feel about myself. Like it's bullshit. Like it's gonna end tomorrow."

I cut in. "Like you're really that poor little kid up there on that screen?"

"Yeah, and like somebody's gonna find out I'm that little kid."

"Sam, that little kid lives inside of you. All he ever wanted was for you to do what you just did."

"What's that?"

"To tell him it's okay."

"And now that I have?"

I laughed and shouted, "Hallelujah! You are cured, son."

He raised his eyebrow.

"Sorry, my evangelical background slipped in there for a second. Actually, it's true, but let me put it in different words. He won't bug you anymore. He won't . . . you won't feel like a fake. And when you have an audition, or whatever it is that you do these days, you will know you are the man you've worked your ass off to become. How cool is that?"

He laughed. "Way cool. Seriously, you mean it? No more night sweats, headaches, clammy palms?"

"Nope. In fact, call me as soon as you've tried it out."

Sam did call me. Two days later I received a message on my service: "D, it's Sam. You're cool. It's cool. I am lovin' life, thanks."

*   *   *

The important thing to remember about this phase is that pain is pain, no matter which way you slice it. So, whatever you experienced on your first journey of this phase, it is an integral part of your healing. It doesn't matter how large or how small it may have appeared to you in comparison to Cary, Suzette, or Sam. Or anyone else, for that matter. If your mind recalled that memory, it is an important step in your healing.

Never compare your life to others'. You are what matters to God. You are what is important right here, right now.

What you are allowing yourself to do is heal the past. With phasing you use all of your senses to reconstruct, on the screen in your mind's eye, a different outcome. An outcome where you feel safe, where you feel like someone has stood up for you. Where you are the brave one. You are the heroine or the hero.

It's exactly like deleting an old file from your computer. Why do you delete it? Because you no longer have a need for it. It's useless to you now. It is just taking up space on your computer's memory.

The subconscious mind operates the same way. It will not respond to you unless you feed it the correct codes. When you delete the past by going "in between" worlds, you release the part of you that is no longer needed. That "old file" (that old cellular memory) is deleted and you reconstruct a new file, one that is useful to you now.

The Fork in the Road

We stumble and we fall
From the chances that we take
It doesn't mean we're down for good
There are no mistakes
If you follow what's inside your heart
Believe and finish what you start
Open the door you're inside.

From the song "Have No Fears"
Words by Molly Pasutti

This phase is an added bonus to Phase Three. It is the opportunity to return to a place in the past where, as you look back on your life, you shake your head in defeat, mumbling to yourself, "Why did I choose that? If I had chosen the other path, I would be . . ."

On your powerful journey, as you are soul surfing "between worlds," you have the opportunity to go back to that fork in the road, to run the camera in your mind's eye in reverse. To see why, at the particular time, you made the choice you made.

You will then know that you have the power to change the effects of that choice, right in your cellular makeup where those effects are stored. As we journey into your good old memory banks, you will be able to change the "data" of defeat into the sweet exhilaration of victory.

Let's do it! Let's Rock and Roll!!!

By now, I'm sure you've got the first part: the music, the posture, and your breath. After exhaling the seventh deep breath, start phasing. See the giant screen in front of you. Feel your emotions start to rev. Like the motor of a finely tuned Porsche, you are at the starting line waiting to win this race.

On the giant screen in your mind, see a long road. It is a road you have already journeyed down. Lock on to the screen. Put scenery on each side of the road, if you like. Make the road real in your mind's eye. Focus on that road for a moment. As mixed emotions come up, identify them, but stay focused on that road up there on the screen. You are faintly aware of the music playing in the background. Anticipation is building.

The camera in your mind "pans" that road on the screen. It stops abruptly at a fork in the road. Put yourself up there on that screen—the you of the past at a place in your life where you stood at a fork in the road. Indecision clouds your emotions as you try to choose the right direction. Allow yourself to feel the angst building inside as you ponder which direction to choose, thinking to yourself, *If I go this way . . . If I go that way . . .*

Go back to that time, a time when you made a life-changing decision. The decision you made came from the programming of your Conditioned Destiny. Perhaps then it felt like the right decision, the safe choice.

The moment you made that choice and started down that path, you knew you had chosen the wrong direction. Everything inside of you screamed at the choice you made. But you'd already started down that path, as you told yourself, "Too late to turn back now."

Sighing, you resigned yourself. "Oh, well, what's done is done, better make the best of it."

NOT!!!

Look at the giant screen. The camera is rolling in reverse. It takes you back to that exact moment.

The you that is sitting there, aching for the you on the screen that made that fateful choice, is now standing at the fork in the road. The you of the now and the you of the past acknowledge one another and join hands—becoming one.

This new, powerful you chooses the path inspired by your Divine Spark. Feel the shift in your emotions. From feeling as though you are trapped, plodding along a path that brings you disappointment and frustration, to sprinting down a path where you feel nothing but joy. The course of your life has been changed by that one moment in time. That one decision.

Celebrate!!!

It's no wonder so many people enjoyed the movie *Back to the Future.* How many times have you thought, *If I could just go back and redo it . . . ?*

With Doc's help Michael J. Fox goes back in time. He arrives back when his parents were teenagers. At the ball where his parents met, circumstances are altered by the chain of events that occur that night.

For the first time in his life Michael's father (then a teenager) stands up to the guy that has bullied him his whole life. He shows courage. His Divine Spark compels him to take a stand against Biff, and in doing so, he takes a stand for his life in the future.

You see Michael wake up back in his room, which looks the same. As he rubs his eyes and leaves the bedroom, he does a double take. The entire house looks completely different. His family has been transformed. Instead of being a family of people with lost hope and no self-esteem, each one of them is successful and happy.

The clincher is when he opens the front door to find Biff, his father's persecutor, washing and waxing the family car!

He realizes that by time travel, he has altered the entire future of his family.

I stood, looking out the window of the house I lived in with my first husband. I looked down the street at all the houses exactly alike. I shook my head. There was a deep void inside of me. I felt trapped. I knew there was something so much greater than the life I was living.

As I was staring out the window, this vision came back to me; it was crystal clear in my mind. I saw the revival meeting at Angeles Temple that my father had taken me to, where the lady evangelist prophesied that one day I would be a healer. One day I, too, would take God's message to the world. I remember my evangelist father's angry reaction to those words. I was puzzled. I thought he would be happy I wasn't "full of the devil" like he'd said I was.

Something within me went past the fear of my father's reaction. I knew inside of my young mind what that woman was saying was the truth.

Coming back to the present, I shook my head, turning away from the window, wondering why I had thought of that after all these years.

That one thought was my fork in the road. Within a week after I'd had that recollection, my marriage came crashing to an end.

For two years I fought the destiny I knew I had chosen all along. No matter how much I tried to run from it, my Chosen Destiny was always there in the back of my mind. The harder I fought, the more Spirit would show me what my path was. Looking back on that fateful day so many years ago, when it became crystal clear to me what my Chosen Destiny was, I realize how fortunate I was. Even though life—as I had known it—was shattered into little pieces. Even though, as much as I rebelled, cried, ranted, and raved, it was gone. Even though I fought hard to hold on to my past, it was clear my future was at that fork of the road. What I painfully thought was the end was really an incredible beginning. I now began to use the latent gifts Spirit had blessed me with from birth. The gifts that were thought of as "evil" by my father and his wife became valuable tools to reach deep into lives of the people I've had the privilege to touch.

Janie's excitement filled her voice on the telephone. "Dawnea, I did it. I finally did it. I started taking dance class. I still have my day job, but I've finally taken the first step in doing what I've wanted to do since I was six years old. I can't tell you how much this means to me. I listened to the tape of our session together. The part where you tell me to just take that leap of faith. I did it!"

Eight months earlier Janie had sat in my office staring out at the ocean, hands folded neatly in her lap, legs crossed in an attitude of defense.

I clicked on the cassette recorder and began speaking. "This session is for Janie. Realizing the information coming forth is for her best and highest good, and being blessed with the free human will to change anything we may hear." I wondered to myself how many times I'd spoken those words in years past.

I closed my eyes for a moment, took a deep breath, and began speaking. As usual "the Voice" was speaking through me as I started to describe to Janie what I was seeing, feeling, and hearing: "Janie, you are trapped. It's as though you are in a cage. The key to the cage is right there within your reach. But you are afraid to reach for it. I feel this has to do with your creativity, not your love life. Correct?" I looked over at her. Tears were starting to form in the corners of her eyes; she was bit-ing her lip anxiously. She didn't speak—just nodded her head in agreement.

I debated with myself: Should I continue talking, simply telling Janie what I was seeing, feeling, and hearing about her, or should I use phasing as a way of letting her reexperience that time when her choice was to lock herself into a cage of her own design?

"Phasing, definitely," I said to myself.

"Janie, listen, I want to take you on a little journey. Are you okay with that?"

Her eyes were full of questions, but she grudgingly agreed.

"Good. This will be on tape so you can use it later. Now, sit up straight, unfold your arms, uncross your legs. Take a deep breath and relax. . . ." I began, as I took Janie through the prep work to begin phasing.

"Janie, now I want you to see a giant screen in your mind. The kind of screen you see at the movies. Do you see the giant screen, Janie?"

Her soft, timid voice spoke: "Yes, I do, Dawnea."

"Good. Now . . . on that screen I want you to see a road. The road is long and winding. You come to a large fork in this road. You are back at a time in your life where you had a choice to make. For whatever reason, you chose the road that was not your true choice. It was the choice of compromise. Janie, are you in this place?"

In a stronger voice she answered me instantly, "Oh, yes, I'm right there."

"When was that choice made, Janie?"

"Right out of high school. I wanted to major in dance

in college. I have been dancing since I was four years old. I love it. I starred in every dance program our small dance school put on. When I was on that stage, I felt like someone. I danced all through high school. My parents—well, my mother—always came to see me perform. But Dad, he thought it was a waste of my brain. He wanted me to major in law just like him."

Janie began wringing her hands together. I glanced at her and saw that her face was tight; anger was written all over it.

"Janie, what happened? Did you major in dance?"

Her voice broke as she confessed, "No, I did what Dad wanted. I majored in law . . . and I hated every damn minute of it. I still do."

Then the dam broke: "I hate my life. Damn it, I want out of this cage. I want out of it, do you hear me? Let me out!!!" Tears of frustration poured out of Janie.

"Janie, do you really want out of the cage?" I asked.

"Hell, yes, I do," she confirmed.

"Janie, see the key to the cage lying there? Pick it up, unlock the door, and walk out." She was silent for several minutes as I carefully monitored her. (I intuitively watched what she was doing up there on that screen.) Just as I "saw" her dancing, I looked over at her. Her face was beaming; the look of ecstasy on this young woman was amazing. I joined her in joyful tears.

"Janie, what are you doing up there on that screen?"

"I'm dancing, Dawnea, I am dancing."

* * *

My thoughts came back to the phone call.

"Janie, congratulations. I am so happy for you."

"I'm happy for me too. And you know what? I'm still using the phasing tape you made for me. I think that was the key. I haven't given up my day job yet, but I will be in the next performance the class has. Will you come?"

"Yes, I'd love to."

"Dawnea, thank you. I'm out of the cage. I don't know where this is all going, but I'm really enjoying my life."

I smiled to myself and said, "Of course you are. You changed your life by taking that first step. My dear, you are living your Chosen Destiny."

Mark sat across from me, all tension gone from his face. We had just completed the "fork-in-the-road" phasing session.

"Dawnea, you have no idea how good it feels to let go of the guilt as a result of the decision I made back then."

I laughed, saying, "Umm, I think I have a little idea, Mark. I was there with you."

He smiled. "Yes, I saw you there. How strange is that?"

"Stranger than fiction, maybe?"

We both laughed.

"So, now maybe you can really begin to live your life? Allow yourself to receive in this relationship?"

"Yes, I will. I must tell you Lawrence will be grateful

to you. I have put the poor man through hell these last several months."

"Mark, the important thing to remember is, when you live your truth without guilt, that's when you can be happy. You are honoring yourself."

"But it's hard. I mean, I really wanted my marriage to work. And I loved Jessica. Well, I loved her like a friend, but never like a lover. How could I?"

"You couldn't. It's not the way you are made, my dear. Honor that. But, so you don't start doubting yourself and the work we've just done, let's clear this up. Why do you think you made the decision to marry Jessica when you were really in love with Lawrence?"

Mark hesitated in answer to the questions, and I encouraged him: "Come on now, truth here, Mark."

He sighed. "Truth?"

"Yeah, truth," I stated.

"I wasn't ready to come out. And at the time I truly believed I could be married to a woman, that I could make it work. But as soon as the wedding was over—well, actually during the ceremony, when they ask that question, you know, 'Is there any reason why these two should not be together,' my stomach knotted. I knew it was a lie. I kept seeing Lawrence's face, but . . . I just couldn't call the whole thing off; I mean my family, her family . . ."

I looked over at Mark—he was wringing his hands. I gently said, "Mark, it's okay. Now we have finished this. Those little nagging doubts as to whether you could ever be happy with Jessica will not be there. Who you are, who you really are, is out in the open. Doesn't that feel good?"

His eyes were shining, as he nodded his head in agreement.

"Whew, what a relief. That poor man—me—on that screen. It was clear how he was fighting everything in his life. My God, it's good to be free of all of that."

Looking at Mark, I was once again reminded how brave people can be.

"Mark, I think you owe Lawrence dinner out tonight. What do you say?"

"Yes, all that and more. Oh, one more thing."

"Yes."

"He'll want to book a session with you."

I laughed and replied, "Right on. You know the number."

He looked at me with those big blue eyes and whispered, "Yeah, I know the number by heart."

I did work with Lawrence a month later. It was clear in the session how much his relationship with Mark had improved. Mark was able to communicate, to allow Lawrence to nurture him. Obviously, the guilt was gone.

About *Back to the Future.* I hear you thinking, *Come on, now, Dawnea, that was a movie, make-believe. It can't happen in "real life."*

Yes and no. No, as far as I know, no one has invented

a car that will travel either forward or backward in time. As of now, you cannot physically go back and alter the events of the past that will lead to a different future.

However, you can use the screen in your mind to go back in between worlds (phasing) to re-create that past for yourself emotionally.

Think about what I've told you regarding the subconscious mind. It doesn't know the difference between "real-life experience" and the experience of phasing. The subconscious mind connects to the conscious mind through your emotions. If your emotions are telling the subconscious mind that you are no longer a victim, you no longer are; indeed, you are reclaiming your Divine birthright, your Chosen Destiny. The subconscious mind has no other choice but to respond to what your emotions are feeding it. In the words of a dear friend of mine, "Karma ends when you 'get it.'"

So get busy. Time to look at your inner computer. Time to throw out those old files. Time to build new ones!!!

I want you, like Janie and Mark, to go back to that fork in the road and stand there. Then choose the road that leads to your happiness, your joy, and your completion. In other words, live your bliss.

Oh, one more thing: In recent years there has been so much talk about "healing the inner child." It has been on every talk show, a big part of the psychological "buzz" for quite a while. Obviously, I agree with this. That's what Phase Three is all about. However, I *do not* agree that you should be stuck there. Once you've phased it, journaled it, then *let it go.* Move on to the next mountain in your life. Don't spend the rest of your life moving the same old shit around.

Your reality is where your consciousness is, so when you have phased it, blessed it, blessed them (whoever "they" are), and—I'll say it again—get out of your pissy diapers. Stop feeling sorry for yourself. Take back your power and move on!!!

Courage Under Fire

*"The lion takes its fierceness
from your fear. Walk up to the lion
and he will disappear;
run away
and he runs after you."*

The Game of Life and How to Play It
by Florence Scovel Shinn

When you finish Phase Four, you are going to know you are free. Free of the thing that keeps every human being from living his or her life in the Chosen Destiny. Free of *fear*.

We humans are motivated by two main emotions. They are love and fear. If you think about it, all of our other emotional responses are based on these two powerful emotions.

As you cut the ties with the deep-seated fear that is presently stored inside of you, you will feel yourself strongly connected to your Divine Spark. You will know the fear is gone—that it no longer has its negative hold on you. You *will* be free!!!

*   *   *

Sit erect and comfortably. Allow yourself to drop into the rhythm of your breathing—in through your nose, holding the breath, letting it go out through your mouth. Your body and your emotions know you are entering into phasing. Even though you may feel relaxed after the count of three or four, continue on until you have completed the entire seven cycles of breath.

As you draw in, hold, and release your seventh breath, see the giant screen in front of you. All of your senses are focusing on that giant screen in your mind's eye.

A white room appears on the screen. You can barely distinguish the walls from the door. The room is completely empty, except for two chairs.

Put yourself on the screen. See yourself as you are right now, entering the room. Sit down in one of the chairs.

Feel yourself dropping into the pattern of your breathing. You are a little nervous, anticipation is rising, but you continue to sit in the chair—breathing in through your nose, holding the breath to the count of seven, and out through your mouth.

The door opens and someone enters the room. Direct your attention to this person. What are they wearing? How tall are they? What color is their hair? Their eyes? The image on the screen is larger than life. What do you feel when you look at them?

This person sits down across from you. He or she is intently staring at you. Unnerving as it may be, you drum up the courage to ask, "Who are you and why are you here?"

At first there is silence. Your companion just sits there, staring at you with eyes that do not blink.

Impatience rises within you and you shout, "Hey, I'm asking you who you are!"

Calmly, the person folds their hands in their lap and bows their head. And there the two of you sit for several moments. Perplexed, you decide to wait it out. The next move is theirs.

After several moments pass, the person raises their head, looks you straight in the eye, and says, "I am your fear. I am the part of you that will not let you make any changes in your life. I am the part of you that is afraid to chance it, afraid to try, afraid to trust, afraid to live. I am your fear." Then it dawns upon you: The person sitting across from you is an aspect of yourself!

What is your reaction to this? As you sit across from this person, this deep, dark part of yourself—your fear—what are you thinking? What are you feeling? Don't even dream of holding back; let your emotions come rushing forward. You are facing the very thing that has kept you from having what it is in life you deeply, truly desire. You are looking your fear in the face.

At this moment you are Mel Gibson in *Braveheart*. You are facing your biggest enemy and your strongest teacher. Go with it.

On the white wall behind that dark part of you, your fear, scenes from the past go racing by. All of the times you have backed down, all of the times you have compromised, all of the times you said no when you wanted to say yes, or yes when you really wanted to say no, are playing larger than life.

The whole gamut of experience, from the smallest memory of defeat to the deepest desire you have not yet manifested, is passing by in front of you on that white wall. All parts of you, the you on the screen *and* the you watching, are reliving the many times you wanted to try but fear overtook you. See those times clearly. See it all. Feel it. Feel it with all the stored-up emotion you have locked inside.

Let it all come up *now*!!!

As your emotions surface, something begins to stir deep inside you. As you watch the images of the past, the Conditioned Destiny voice inside tells you about all your failures, but the Divine Spark within you rises up.

The you on the screen jumps up out of the chair; in one step you are standing nose-to-nose with your fear. You command it to leave this room, leave your life. This deciding moment of confrontation is life-changing! You have just taken back your power! Your fear has vanished. The room is empty except for you. You won!!

By taking control of your fear, the tape you have been listening to that said, *I'll never get there, I'll never have my deepest desires, I can't succeed. I cannot become the person I want to be. I can't do it—I can't do it at all,* is over.

The you on the screen is standing in the room, victorious, with tears of joy pouring from your eyes. The you, sitting and watching, is in complete rapport with the you on the screen. Emotions are swirling through you. The Divine Spark rises within you. The part of you that has been locked behind your fear— buried deep inside of you—rises up and shouts, "Freedom!"

You raise your arms high in the air and shout, "Victory!!"

You know with everything within you that there is no other outcome now. That freedom to live your life as you have ached to for as long as you can remember is now yours.

The white room disappears. In its place is a new movie. The you on the screen is living those dreams you stored away so long ago behind that old fear that said you could not have it, could not be it. A larger-than-life picture of those dreams is playing right there—on that giant screen inside you. Your emotions are sparking. The emotional live wires within you have been reconnected.

Your success has become the living, breathing essence of you. All of your emotions are locked in to the scene of victory. Scene by triumphant scene is running on the giant screen of your mind. Sit back down in the chair and watch as your life unfolds right in front of your eyes—the life you have always known you were meant to live.

Stay with your internal victory for a moment. You have done monumental work. Being "in between" worlds is not always easy. The phasing you have just completed is a major step in reclaiming your Divine heritage. Savor it!!!

Throughout the movie *Flashdance* you watch Alex (Jennifer Beals) battling with her fear as she tries to turn her dream into a reality: the dream that she will one day attend the Royal Academy of Dance. Her mentor, Hanna, encourages her, tells her she can do it. Frightened as she is, the hunger to see her dream a reality spurs her on. Alex focuses on that dream.

The first scene in which you see Alex addressing her fear of failure, of *not* getting accepted into the academy, is when she walks into the dance academy after working her day job as a welder. She is dressed in army clothes and boots. The camera flashes to the feet of the people standing in line. Most of them are shod in ballet slippers or dance shoes of some sort. She's in her army boots. Alex fidgets while she waits her turn in line. The prissy dancers around her are looking down their noses at her. The closer she gets to the woman behind the desk handing out applications, the more nervous she becomes. Suddenly, it all becomes too overwhelming for Alex. She turns, runs out of the academy, and gets on her bicycle. She rides for her life.

The movie continues to show us her inner and outer battles. Finally, she has her audition before the board of the academy. She walks in—this little dancer who never had any formal training—as the camera pans the faces of the panel. You can see them looking down their noses, saying to themselves, *Let's get it over with.*

The music starts, Alex begins to dance, and she slips. She stops, takes a deep breath, and then asks to start over.

As you watch, you can see her concentration deepen and a fierce determination take over, as she focuses herself for that one moment in her life. And she does it. She dances her ass off.

Those stuffy, conservative people are clapping and tapping their feet, looking on in amazement as Alex dances for her life. Dances for her Chosen Destiny.

For the last month Divine Mind has been prompting me to see my father. It's been years, but that thing deep inside of me would not let up. Talk about confronting my deepest fear! On that giant screen in my mind I watched as the different parts of myself were waging battle against each other. The part of me that trusted, that knew I had to do this thing, was winning. All this while I was rolling down the freeway, heading toward my father's house. I had made the decision to use my telepathy as a profession. Something in me felt as though I had to tell him what I was about to do. I know this sounds a little bizarre, but I wanted to thank him for the training I had received in those revival meetings.

Even though I did not believe in what my father did, I felt those years spent with him were invaluable training for the work I was about to do. I still believe it. There have been so many times when, during client sessions, someone has a powerful breakthrough, that I get tears in my eyes. When that happens, I say to myself, *Daddy, I wish you could see this. This is what* real *healing is all about. It is about giving love,* not *teaching fear.*

Though I would not have admitted it that day so long ago, I also had the wild idea I would get his approval for what I was about to do with my life. I had telephoned ahead. I related the reason for my visit to my step-mother. She refused to allow me to speak to my father. That was nothing new; my stepmother never allowed me to speak to my father on the phone, she had this thing about "protecting him" from outsiders. (Me being one of those, in her mind.)

As I pulled into the driveway, beads of sweat trickled down the back of my neck. Memories, horrible memories of past abuses, raced through that giant screen in my mind. I turned the motor off in my little blue bug, closed my eyes, took a deep breath, and willed myself to relax. "It's okay," I told myself out loud, "you are coming from a place of love." Even though I said those words, even though I knew they were true, I couldn't help remembering all the times of degradation and criticism.

Taking another deep breath, I stepped out of the car and headed for the front door.

The door swung open before I reached it. There stood my stepmother, eyes glaring. My heart raced; I was a grown woman, but let me just tell you, the little girl inside was scared shitless. "Is Daddy here?" I asked.

She sneered, saying, "Devil, you have a lying tongue. How dare you come to your father's house thinking you can bring Satan in the door? I won't have it."

I took a weary breath as I thought about how many times I had been accused of being full of the devil. Of *being* Satan himself. "Look, Momma, I came to talk to Daddy. I want to thank him for the things he taught me," I placatingly offered.

Her eyes narrowed into slits as she continued, unconvinced. "Oh, yeah, use God's holy word for Satan. Get off my porch, devil! Get away from here—go!" Then she slammed the door in my face.

Tears rolled down my face as I walked to my car. Oh, how my heart ached. I was about one block away when the emotional dam broke. I pulled my car over and wept long and hard. I wept for all the lost years and all the pain. I couldn't stop myself; I didn't want to. The faucet was on, so I just let it run. I finally took a last gulping breath, started my car, and drove away. As I entered the freeway, a horrible anger rose within me. And there I am, driving down the freeway, screaming at the top of my lungs, "Okay, Divine Mind, what the hell was that? I know you prompted me to go see my father—what exactly got accomplished today? I'm a wreck."

All I heard was silence.

I shouted again, "I said, 'I am a wreck.'"

The silence repeated itself.

"Well, shit," I muttered. A thought crept into my head: Maybe it was me, *not* Divine Mind, that prompted that visit; maybe the part of me that needed Daddy's validation, something I had to be insane to believe I would get. But I knew the difference between my voice and Divine Mind's voice. Didn't I? (Conditioned Destiny rearing its head.)

Two days later I was on the 405 freeway, near the Sunset off-ramp, when I heard Divine Mind's voice tell me, "Slow down and look in your rearview mirror." I looked; several cars back in the slow lane was my father. I couldn't make out his face, but I knew it was him. My heart started to race as I changed lanes and then slowed way down. I was moving at a snail's pace as my eyes were glued to the rearview mirror, waiting for him to come up alongside me. After what seemed like an eternity, he was two cars behind me, one lane over. Needless to say, I was freaked out. The thought of confronting my father after all this time made my hands sweat; my heart was thumping loudly in my chest, my throat was dry and constricted. "Okay, girl, just relax," I said with a courage I did not feel. I took a deep breath and requested, "Divine Mind, be with me now. Help me to see through your eyes, through the eyes of truth."

Something inside me shifted. I felt a calm wave wash over me. I knew I had to see him. I had to look him in the eyes.

Finally, he was next to me. I tooted my horn and he turned and looked me dead in the eyes. You know how it is when you think time can stand still? That was this moment in my life. It was a brief moment, but that moment did so much for me. He looked at me—dead on—blue eyes facing blue eyes. Then he nodded his head ever so slightly. The telepath in me knew what that slight nod meant. He was saying he knew about my visit to his house. As I looked into his face, I sensed something else: regret. Then it was gone. He was gone. He had accelerated, leaving me to my thoughts. I was shaken, deeply shaken. I pulled off at the next off-ramp and sobbed. So much was said in those brief moments. He was unguarded, I saw it on his face. He knew the path I had chosen. And on some level my father knew his part in that choice. Divine Mind had prompted me to make that journey to his house. I took a deep breath, determined to continue to live my Chosen Destiny.

As Melissa walked into my office and sat down, I had to do a double take.

She saw my reaction and smiled, saying, "I'm not the

same woman I was when you saw me eight months ago, am I, Dawnea?"

I smiled back, awed by the transformation in Melissa. "You look like you've gotten your power back. Do you want to tell me about it?"

"I don't know if you remember our last session. Two things you said triggered me. One was the part about facing my fear. The fear that kept me from having the body I wanted, the self-confidence I craved. The other was that, locked inside me, was the person I desired to be. You said that if I could see it clearly in my mind and if I knew I deserved it, there was nothing in the world that could keep it from me."

Our last session together came rushing into my mind. Melissa had been at least forty pounds heavier. She had been angry—so angry at life. The ripples of frustration wafted off her body, filling my office. I'd had to do deep breathing to keep myself from choking on her rage and frustration.

"Yes, I remember that day vividly."

"Dawnea, what really kept me going was the phasing session we did. Every time I would feel frustrated and want to stuff myself, I would put on the tape of that session."

The image of that day in the treatment room was clear in my mind. I saw Melissa on the treatment table, heard the music playing in the background, as my voice gently spoke to her: "Melissa, I want you to see the you of today. See it up there on that giant screen in your mind. There is a reason you are in this place, there is a reason why you have allowed your body to become what it is. What is that reason?"

Hearing only silence, I watched as Melissa's fists clenched in anger. I waited several moments, then coaxed her on. "Melissa, you can do this. What's going on up there on that screen? What are your emotions doing? Tell me, Melissa, tell me now."

She took a ragged breath through her clenched teeth and spat out, "I hate my mother. I hate her so much. I hate what she did to me."

I put my hand on Melissa's heart. "Melissa, what did your mother do?"

She pounded her fists on the table, crying out, "I was never good enough. Never smart enough, never pretty enough, and never thin enough." Then she laughed this little rebellious laugh. "So I got even with her."

"What did you do?"

"I started stashing sweets in my room. I would hide them everywhere. Chocolate bars, Twinkies, Snowballs—anything I could get my hands on. I even stole money out of Mom's purse to buy them. Each time she would pass the bread basket by me and to my brother at the dinner table, I would secretly plot how many candy bars I would eat later on. I got even with her!"

"Did you, Melissa? Did you get even with Mom?"

She was quiet for a moment, then she started to cry. "It backfired. All I really wanted was love and support, and after a while the food couldn't give it to me. By then I couldn't stop myself. Each time I had a disappointment, I would go back to the little girl who stashed her candy. But it's empty, so very empty."

Melissa began to cry; deep, painful sobs escaped her. "I feel so stupid, I feel so defeated. I am so alone. I didn't get even with my mother, I trapped myself. I'm trapped by my own anger, by my own fear that I will fail. I've tried diet after diet and proven I can't do it. I fail every time . . . every time."

I put both of my hands on Melissa's heart. I could feel the raw pain escaping from her. I let her cry it all out.

I leaned down and whispered in Melissa's ear, "Melissa, I want you to see yourself as you are right now. You're so brave. You have come here and you are facing that deep, wounded part of you. I want you to give yourself a hug."

Slowly she wrapped her arms around herself.

"Good. Now, and most important, I want you to tell yourself, 'Diets do not work!!' They set you up to fail because they're founded on deprivation."

She repeated the words I had said, then she repeated them again. The third time she repeated my words, her voice was strong. She was taking back her power; I could hear it in her voice. Her fists unclenched.

"Now I want you on that giant screen in front of you, Melissa. On that screen in your mind I want you to see yourself as you are right at this moment. See the radiance shining from your eyes. Feel your heart responding to the Divine Spark within you. You are a Child of the Universe. You can do whatever you put your mind to. You can be anything you choose.

"I want you to acknowledge that at this very moment, you—just as you are—are perfect." Melissa shook her head in disagreement.

Gently, yet firmly, I took her hand, explaining, "Yes, Melissa, you are perfect. There is only one perfect you on this planet. Acknowledge that. Right now, this moment, see on the screen in your mind how brave you are, how strong you can be, and how beauty is something that happens inside of you. You are a perfect Child of the Universe, a reflection of the Divine, and you are loved exactly as you are."

Tears were running down Melissa's face as I continued. "Healing your life does not come from having a skinny body. It comes from owning your own power. So do it, Melissa, do it now!!!"

I waited several moments; I wanted those words to soak in.

"Now see yourself on the screen in your mind. See yourself how *you choose* to be. How you choose to look, how you choose to dress, how you choose to live your life. While you are seeing the picture on the screen in your mind, hook your emotions into this picture. Your emotions are the juice, the wellspring, that gives the picture that is running on that giant screen life. Your emotions are the key to making the picture real in the world outside of this room."

I let Melissa work with herself for several moments. I could see her breath moving softly and the energy around her body changing. I knew the Work was being done.

"Melissa, allow the screen to disappear. Keep all you have just seen, felt, and experienced deep inside of you."

I blinked myself back to today, smiled at Melissa sitting across from me, and said, "Yes, that was a powerful session."

"Dawnea, there's more. I actually was able to forgive my mother. I stopped blaming her. I took responsibility for my own actions, my own life. God, it feels so good to be free!!!"

I was surprised when I received the call from Becca saying she wanted a follow-up session. Two days before, she had experienced one of the most powerful phasing sessions I'd ever worked with. I pondered why she was coming in. When I focused my meditation on her, I saw clearly what had happened.

I opened the doors to my office to greet her. "Becca, come in."

Hesitantly, she followed me into my office. I motioned for her to sit down.

I looked her in the eyes, and she avoided my gaze. Silently, I shook my head, thinking, *Old patterns die hard.*

"So, Becca, what's up?"

"Well, remember how you said the critic might flare up? The part of me that thinks I made the whole thing up?"

"Yeah, I remember that. So?"

"Well, what if I did make it up? What if the phasing we did wasn't really real? What if—"

I stopped her in midsentence. "Becca, let me ask you a question." I looked straight at her as I asked, "Do you want to be happy, really happy?"

She stuttered, "Well, yes . . . yes, of course I do."

I put up my hand and replied, "Just checking. Go on. . . ."

She continued. "Anyway, so this critic in me—"

I shot back, "Is it the voice of your Conditioned Destiny that says, 'You can't do it? You can't do it at all? Becca, you cannot have happiness'? Becca, when you were phasing, did you feel the emotion of what you were seeing on that screen?"

"Yes, I did."

"Did your body respond to those emotions?"

She paused, then said, "Yes, I felt it way down to my toes. I especially felt it in my heart."

I sighed and told her, "The body does not lie. Nor do your emotions."

"But I can't—"

I held up my hand, stopping her dead in midsentence again.

"Okay, close your eyes—right now—close them."

She did.

"Now take a deep breath, let it out, and now another." I took her through seven circular breaths.

"Now I want you to see a room. An empty white room. You are sitting in that room. Someone opens the white door, sits across from you. Who are they? What do they look like?"

"It's a woman. A beautiful woman with long cascading hair. She's wearing a long flowing dress. Her face is radiant with love."

"Ask her who she is, Becca."

"Who are you?" she asks.

"What does she say?" I prompted her.

"She says she's me. The part of me I've never allowed myself to become."

"What do you want to do with this beautiful woman, Becca?"

"I want to be her."

"Then do it. Both of you rise from your chairs. Stand and face each other, eye-to-eye, heart-to-heart. Now feel yourself merging with her. Feel yourself becoming one with your own beauty."

I waited for several moments, holding Becca's image of herself in my mind. I asked Divine Mind to touch Becca; to allow Becca to feel what unconditional love was all about. No sooner had I asked this than Becca opened her eyes as tears of joy streamed down her face.

"Dawnea, I felt it. I felt us merge. And then I felt something touch my heart. It filled me with something . . . something I'd never felt.

"Is it as easy as this?" she wondered out loud.

I smiled and said, "Yes, it is this easy. In fact, it is so easy, most people miss it. They think they have to suffer greatly. Well, they don't. You don't.

"Becca, every time the voice of your fear tries to raise its ugly head, I want you to see this part of you."

I looked at this brave young woman. "Congratulations, Becca, welcome to your life."

She smiled.

Jeremy was in a total state of frustration. He'd been to see me several times in the last two years. I'd never seen him this distraught.

"Dawnea, I've submitted the proposal for my movie, *And They Run,* to all the festivals. I've been turned down by all of them."

"All of them, Jeremy?"

"Okay, there's two more. I'm panicking. This has got to happen this year."

"Jeremy, relax."

He raised his perfectly formed eyebrows. "Easy for you to say."

"Why don't we phase and find out what the problem is."

"I don't know if I can phase today. I just want you to tell me it's going to be okay. Tell me that one of these bastards will take my script."

"Nope. That would be the easy way out. I want you to *see* it. See it on that movie screen in your mind."

He crossed his arms over his chest, scowling at me.

I ignored it. "Ready?" I asked.

Through clenched teeth he spat, "I guess so."

"Good, let's get started."

As soon as Jeremy did his third round of circular breathing, he completely relaxed. (What'd I tell you? Who needs drugs?)

"Jeremy, see the giant screen in front of you. See a white room on that screen. See yourself in that room. Someone is in there, Jeremy. Who is it?"

"It's my father."

"What is your father doing?"

"He's drunk. He's pointing his big fat finger at me. Says I'll never be the filmmaker he is. Never."

Jeremy was silent, his breathing heavy and labored.

"Jeremy, what are you doing now?"

"I'm looking at this horrible man. He is my fear. His voice is the voice that says I can't make it as a screenwriter. That I won't make it in the industry."

"Are you willing to let that voice win? Let *him* win, Jeremy?"

"I don't want to, but . . ."

"But what? Jeremy, I want you to walk up to him and I want you to tell him you know why he's doing this. I want you to tell him you know he's scared to death. Scared you will be better than him. That you have more talent than him. I want you to look him in the eye and tell him this now!!!"

There were a few moments of silence, then . . . Jeremy's laughter. "You're right, Dawnea. As you were saying those words, he started shrinking. He became the incredible shrinking man. Fuck, that is so cool. I never saw it before. It's truth. The absolute truth. Fuck him. I am going to sell this damn script. I see myself doing it."

Jeremy opened his eyes. He was grinning from ear to ear.

A few weeks went by. One morning, as I picked up my messages, Jeremy's voice greeted me. "Dawnea, just thought you'd like to know my film got accepted by the festival in Europe. I'm so excited. I have you to thank for it. You and phasing."

What happened to Jeremy, Melissa, and Becca was so powerful! Each, in their own way, faced and slew their lion of fear. With phasing you, too, can do this. When the truth becomes crystal clear to you, you will act on it. You have no choice, really. Your Chosen Destiny has kicked in. The Divine Spark is fanning the flames of your courage.

When you allow yourself to be given the "kiss of truth," that is your fork in the road. You allow yourself to break through all of your past conditioning. That's when you can and will claim your Chosen Destiny.

I Want It, I Want It All!!!

You do the Work, you get the Goodies. . . .

The Intraphase Workshops, 1987

In this phase, before we begin your journey, I want to give you a few pointers.

Lacking anything in your life is denying your Divine birthright.

Since the Universe is all-abundant, so should your life reflect that abundance. Are you not a Child of the Universe? People who preach that it is "spiritual to be poor" are negating that very thing the Universe is.

Look up at the stars on a clear night. What do you see? Can you count them? Can you even fathom how many there are? That vastness, that magnitude, that abundance, is Divine energy manifested.

Phase Five is about owning your power in the material world you live in. It is about manifesting your deepest desire. Be it a new house, a new car, an entire new life, the career you've always dreamed of but never had the nerve to go after, that trip you've always longed to take but told yourself, *Oh, I can't do that. I can't afford that.* (That's the voice of the Conditioned Destiny kicking you in the gut.)

Phase Five is about manifestation! With every phase of the soul-surfing process it is important to have all of your senses attached to the journey. In this phase you must also be deeply connected to your desire for the thing you are about to manifest. The degree in which you are "hooked" into that burning desire within you will determine how much, and how quickly, that thing will manifest in your life outside of phasing, that is, the world you live in every day.

I mean, you've got to want it with every part of you. Every single nerve ending. You have got to want it so much, it is the only thing you see and feel.

Okay, ready? Let's do it!!!

As you are sitting there ready to slip into phasing, I want you to scan your soul to single out the one thing in your life that is missing. It must be the most important thing to you. *That one all-important thing!*

Lock it in your mind, take a deep breath, and see the giant movie screen appear before you. You appear on the screen— larger than life. The you of this exact moment is standing on that screen. In front of you appears an iridescent door. You are slightly apprehensive, so for safety's sake, put your arm through the door. As you draw it back, your arm has the same glowing iridescence. You notice that your arm has also started to feel tingly, a sensation so soothing, you want to walk right through that shimmery door. So do it. Step right on through.

You are now standing in a room filled with iridescent light. You feel as if you are floating. There is no time and no space. You just are. You think to yourself, *I'd like a glass of water.* The water appears in front of you in a beautiful silver goblet, bedecked with precious gems. You take a drink of the water; you feel its shimmery energy all through your body. You slip into a stronger rapport with yourself. In this room, thoughts are things. As soon as you soak in that awareness, see yourself on the screen closing your eyes. With eyes closed you see the thing you want most in your life. As you open your eyes, it appears in the room with you. From this moment on you are living it.

Like the water in the goblet that so quenched your thirst, this deep desire you manifested quenches your inner longing. Allow yourself to absorb the sensation.

You are observing yourself on that screen. A profound feeling of acknowledgment of your own power to manifest what you truly desire in this life—life in the now, life here on earth—is rushing through your mind, your emotions, and your body.

Take it a step farther. See and feel the thing that you have just manifested in your day-to-day life. It has already happened. You own it, you are living it right now!!!

Take as long as you need to lock this into the deepest part of you. Feel the exhilaration that comes from knowing you have manifested your deepest desire. That it is in your life from this moment on. That nothing and no one can take it away!!!

When I was a little girl, I loved to watch Shirley Temple. In the movie *The Little Princess* Shirley was in a boarding school. No one could locate her father. Everyone but Shirley thought he was dead.

There was a scene where she and her little friend were up in the attic on Christmas Eve. Both sets of eyes were glowing as they pretended that when they woke up, the room would be cozy from a warm fire; that they would have soft slippers to put on their feet and warm robes to wrap themselves in. And there would be a grand feast for them to eat.

A wealthy old gentleman saw them playing make-believe, and while they were sleeping, he made their pretending a reality.

Whenever I think of their little faces, enraptured by the idea that their wishes—their desires not yet mani-fested—had made the attic warm and the slippers ap-pear, and had caused the grand feast that was laid before them to materialize, I get tears in my eyes. The truth is, their wishes did make it happen.

And so may it be for you.

Let me tell you how I managed to move to Malibu.

Years ago, after my divorce left me shattered finan-cially, I was supporting my two young daughters by working two jobs and doing sessions. The girls and I lived in a little apartment in Canoga Park. On Saturday mornings I would pack my two little daughters in my old green Ford Pinto. We would drive over Topanga Can-yon and out to Malibu. I would take them to the beach. Looking up at the houses, I would say to the girls, "It won't always be like this. Someday, we will live in Malibu and Mommy will drive a nice car, not one that's always breaking down."

As I closed my eyes, feeling the sun on my face and hearing the waves in the background, I saw the giant screen in my mind. On that screen I saw myself walk through that iridescent door and into that room of shimmering light. I would see myself and the girls living in Malibu. Sometimes, it was so powerful that the tears would run down my face.

Even though I did not have the funds to make that move, I would get the local Malibu paper and circle the ads that were right on the water. There was no doubt in my mind that someday I would be coming "home." The home I live in now overlooks the same beach I used to visit with my girls.

I have seen so many of my clients live their dreams. It is hard to pick one story out of the many, but there is one young man who stands out in my mind. It was back in the old days, when I first started doing sessions. I was working a psychic fair in Palo Alto; the day was almost over. I had done over forty sessions that day and I was fried. I felt like I had skid marks on my brain. This angry young man pulled out the chair with his boot and plopped down in front of me. He folded his hands on the table and glared at me with dark, troubled eyes.

Ugh, I thought to myself, *great, I am fried and here's this little punk wanting me to prove I've got chops.* I was just irritated enough to give him an earful. I didn't even ask his name. I took a deep breath and blurted out, "It doesn't take a telepath to see how frustrated you are. It's written all over your face. So why don't you do us both a favor? Go buy yourself a guitar and learn to play it."

Well, let me tell you, the kid turned white as a sheet. "Hey, lady, did my mom tell you that I wanted a guitar?"

I wanted to laugh, but I was too tired. I asked him, "Who's your mom? Listen . . . what's your name?"

With a smirk on his face he answered, "Stage or real?"

My patience was wearing thin as I fired back, "First off, you've never been onstage; and second, I don't care what name you use and neither does the Universe. You've got it all over you, so stop making excuses and blaming your mother. Get a job, buy a guitar, and learn to play. The rest will come."

"What do you mean I got it all over me," he said as he glanced down at my business cards, "—Duana?"

Becoming more irritated, I shot back at him, "My name is Dawnea, like the early-morning sun, with an *e* and an *a*.

"Fame," I continued. (I wanted to add, "you arrogant little fool," but I refrained.) "You've got the vibration of fame all over you. You must have incarnated in with it. But it doesn't come easy, and it's hard to handle once it happens. So do it and realize what you are asking for."

The timer went off. Despite my irritation the healer in me kicked in. I gently touched his hands and said, "These have been given to you as a gift from the Divine

Creator. Go out there and touch the folks with your music."

Shaking his head, he got up out of his chair and walked off. As I was getting in my car, he came up to me. "Hey, do you have a card or something?"

I rolled my eyes, reached in my bag, and handed him my card. "An in-office session is more than ten dollars, you know."

With that same little smirk on his face he said, "Hey, I'm gonna be famous. Money is no object."

The better part of a year went by. I no longer needed to work psychic fairs. I had a full-time practice. One morning I was checking my messages when I heard, blaring out of the answering machine, an amazing guitar riff. Then this raspy voice saying, "Guess who?"

The next morning, same thing—only, this time, "I got the money, you got the time?" Then he left his phone number. He did not leave his name, and I had no idea who it was.

I dialed the number; a woman answered the telephone.

"Hi, could I speak to the guitar player, please?"

"Oh, you mean my son, Norman?"

Hesitating, I said, "Yes . . . Norman, please."

I could hear her in the background yelling, "Norman, there's a woman on the phone, wants to speak to you."

"Ma, my name is not Norman, not anymore."

"Hello."

I remembered who he was as soon as he said hello. "So what's your stage name?" I asked.

"Jonnie."

"Typical rock-and-roll name. I hear you've learned to play the guitar. Congratulations."

"Yeah, well, I want to see you. It's pretty important."

I booked a session with him for the following week.

When he walked into my small office in Marina del Rey, I realized he looked so much older than he had last time I saw him.

"How can I help you, Jonnie?"

"It's not happening fast enough. I can play, but I don't want to just do clubs, I want a record deal."

"Jonnie, how badly do you want this record deal?"

He looked me dead in the eyes and said, "More than I've ever wanted anything in my life. I have to play, Dawnea, I have to. But there's this voice inside of me."

"What voice?"

Pain filled his face as he told me, "It's the voice of my old man. He says I'm not good enough. I'll never be good enough."

I swallowed in order to control my anger. "Jonnie, no one but you can stop you from succeeding."

I turned on the tape recorder and commanded, "Close your eyes."

"What?"

"I said, 'Close your eyes,' " I repeated.

He closed his eyes. We started phasing. I asked Jonnie to see the giant screen in his mind.

I finished, clicked off the tape recorder, and handed the cassette to Jonnie.

His eyes were glazed. "Man, that was unreal. I was

there, Dawnea, I was playing the Forum. Man, it was so real."

I smiled, held out my arms to hug him, and agreed: "Yeah, I know, I saw it too."

He hooted, "Far-fucking-out, man."

I chuckled. "My sentiments exactly. Call me before you sign anything. I want to make sure you don't get screwed."

Three months later the phone call came. Jonnie had gotten his record deal.

"Uhh, Dawnea, I'm so frustrated, so scared. Two more weeks until I take the bar for the eighth time. I didn't even tell anyone this time. I don't want them to know if I fail."

Linda's dark eyes stared at me, fear and frustration written all over her face. Linda and I had been down a long road together. Her painful divorce, the court battles, the move out of her large home in Bel Air to a condo in Pacific Palisades. And then her mother's illness and death. Yes, the last three years had been challenging for Linda, to say the least.

But she came through it all. And with flying colors, I might add. This is where I see the true results of phasing. When someone is in crisis and breaks free, unfettered emotionally, it makes my heart soar for them.

"Linda, not only can you pass the bar this time, you *will* pass the bar. No excuses. Let's get to work."

I took Linda through her circular breathing. By now

she'd phased so many times, she went into the giant screen in her mind without my prompting her.

"Linda, I want you to see yourself in the room where you are taking your test. Do you see the room?"

"Yes."

"Do you see yourself?"

"Yes, yes, I do."

"Good. Now I want you to see yourself taking the test. See yourself *completely* relaxed. The answers are already in your mind. As you are taking the test, call up the giant screen in your mind. See the answers written on that screen. Simply write down what you are seeing. While you are writing, I want you to notice how calm you are. The answers are there. You know they are correct, your emotions respond with confidence."

I was silent while Linda worked on what I had just given her. Several minutes passed.

"Okay, now see yourself receiving the results of the test. You passed with flying colors! See yourself dialing my number. You are calling me to tell me you passed the bar."

I let that soak in. Linda's eyes were still shut, she was still phasing, but there was a big smile on her face.

I did receive that call from Linda. I answered the phone one day while out in the office writing. Linda's excited voice yelled into the receiver, "Dawnea, guess what?"

I teased her. "Umm, let's see. You won the lottery? Your ex-husband's girlfriend's fake tits popped?"

She laughed. "No, even better. I passed the bar. I did it. It was just like in the phasing session. I saw the answers on the giant screen in my mind and it worked. I finished the test in half the time everyone else did."

"Good for you, Linda. Now go out and celebrate!!!"

"But, Dawnea . . . I don't see how phasing can help me get out of this dead-end job. I've been in the mail room at Paramount for four years. I hate it, but I'm afraid to make any change. What if it doesn't work and then I've lost my income?"

I looked across at Greg's scowling face as he sat hunched over in his chair.

"Greg, wasn't that you who said to me just last week, 'I've got to get out of here. Dawnea, I'm dying in this . . .' What were the words you used?" I put my finger on the side of my face and continued. "Let's see . . . 'this ego-infested cesspit of a going-nowhere job.' Oh, yeah, and then there was the part, 'If I have to kiss another no-talent little dickhead's ass, I am going to puke all over their mail.' " I smiled as I watched Greg squirm. "Wasn't that what you said?"

Sheepishly, he grinned and admitted, "Yeah, yeah, I said it. But that's when I was riding high off my thoughts of getting that soap. You know, I got a callback on the audition. And I did great. Man, I was so perfect for the part of Sergio. Then nothing. Maybe I should just give up and move back to New York. I mean, four goddamn years of nothing."

Compassion flooded me as I looked at Greg. It is tough reaching for that star. It puts calluses on your fingers, but . . . ah, when it happens, it's so glorious.

"Greg, listen. You've never phased with me. We've done phone work, I've done telepathic work with you, let's go deeper. Trust me."

"But I came here today to hear about my future. I mean, I thought the Sergio part was the thing you predicted. So if that's not it, what is?"

"Greg, I'll make you a deal. You phase with me, if we run over I'll still answer your questions. Deal?"

He heaved a heavy sigh and said, "Okay, deal."

"Gregory, I want you to sit up straight in your chair. Feet flat on floor. Hands resting on knees, palms up. Now take a deep breath." I took Greg through his circular breathing, reminding him to surf his soul for the source of pain the healing would be focused on that day. Then onto the giant screen, into the room on the screen in his mind with the iridescent door. "Greg, pick up the goblet and drink, drink of your power. Can you do this for me?"

"Yeah, I feel the goblet in my hand. It's heavy. It's ancient, like the Holy Grail. Yeah, that's exactly it. My Holy Grail."

Spoken like an actor. I smiled to myself and continued. "Good. Now, Gregory, I want you to see yourself already there. See yourself on television. You are actually sitting in your living room watching yourself on TV on the screen in your mind. Feel the thrill that comes from knowing, absolutely knowing, you have made it.

You have grabbed that star and you are holding on to it. Feel this, see this, *own* this now."

I was silent to allow Greg to absorb what I'd just given him.

"Now, Gregory, I want you to see yourself out to dinner. This bubbly young teenage girl approaches you. Bashfully, she asks for your autograph. You give her your best smile, her heart melts as you sign your name on that piece of paper she handed you. I am going to be silent. I want you to continue phasing. I want you to fill in the blanks. See your life as a successful actor as though you were already living it. And connect your emotions to what you are seeing. I want you to see it, feel it, breathe it. Do this now!!!"

Several moments went by, then I told him, "Gregory, when you've finished phasing, allow the screen in your mind to disappear. Open your eyes, be present, be in the now."

Greg immediately opened his eyes and said, "Dawnea, that was so powerful. Man, I was there. I was living it. And that part about the girl, well, I saw her right before you started describing her. Man, that was so weird. I feel like I could seriously take on the world right now."

"Greg?"

"Yeah?"

"Go out there and do it!!!"

"Dawnea, one more thing."

Ugh, don't tell me he's going to ask about his future after that, my mind said.

"Just wanted you to know I don't have any questions."

A year went by. I saw Greg every few months. Each time I saw him, he was landing better and better parts.

One day, there was a knock on my door. The local florist handed me a beautiful spring arrangement. I wondered who they were from.

The card read,

Dawnea,
   I love you. I love phasing. I got a costarring role in the show I saw in my phasing session with you. I am on my way.
   Love, Gregory

For those of you who are thinking, *This sounds like a fairy tale, it can't possibly happen for me,* my answer to you is: That's why it hasn't happened for you. Stop that stinkin' thinkin'!!

What was it the Master Jesus said? "According to your faith, be it unto you."

At this moment you are an accumulation of all of the thoughts that run through your mind. So, if the majority of your thoughts are *I can't have it, I can't do it, I don't deserve it,* that's exactly where your life is. Isn't it?

The phasing you have just completed is one of the most powerful journeys Spirit has ever given me. You've just read about Jonnie, Linda, and Greg. You've read how phasing got me a house on Malibu Beach.

What makes you different from us? Your doubt is what makes you different. Get over it!!! Use Phase Five to manifest whatever you want, whatever you feel you need, whatever you know you deserve, in your life. Don't waste any more time. Just get busy!!!

Phase Five and a Half: "Yummy Tidbits"

This is a surefire method to use for those all-important "life-changing" meetings.

Okay, so you've finally got that all-important meeting. It's set for tomorrow morning, 10:00 A.M. sharp. Tiny little shivers of nerves race up and down your spine as you anticipate this meeting. A million things are running through your mind, like . . . What if I don't get it? What if I'm not good enough? *Stop!!!* No wonder you're lying in bed and you can't get to sleep!

Now take a deep breath, let it out. *Calm yourself!!!* How badly do you want this? Is it the opportunity you've been waiting for? How'd you like to "hedge your bets"? Hell, yeah, you say? Well, good. Now we're getting somewhere.

So finish your breathing, see the giant screen in your mind. Now see yourself getting up in the morning, full of energy, ready to go out there and slay that lion called fear. You're ready to claim your Divine birthright. See yourself going through your morning routine. You've already chosen what you will wear. (Never leave these kinds of decisions for the morning.) Teeth brushed, shower taken; you carefully dress; you are out the door and on your way. See yourself walking into that meeting. You smile with confidence at everyone you see that morning. The person you are meeting with greets you. You take their one hand in both of yours. You look them directly in the eye and you say, "I am the one you need. I can do you the most good. I am the only person for this job." Or part, whatever. Then you say to yourself, "I claim this now. I know I want this, I know I am ready for this." (If it were me, I'd be saying, "I got this fucker now. This shit is mine." But then, I tend to get overly excited when I do these things.)

You see yourself in the meeting, full of confidence. Every comment you make is right on target. Every question you are asked you answer in a voice filled with sincerity and knowing— not arrogance, mind you, just the secure knowledge that you are the person they are looking for.

Or, if you are auditioning, you see yourself in that character. You *are* that character. (Same for you musicians and artists. Even us writers.)

Now see yourself calmly shaking the person's hand. You walk out of the building away from prying eyes and you shout, "Thank you! Thank you very much. I nailed this thing. It is mine!!! (Or, you could use my more colorful victorious shouts.)

You are at home or in your hotel room. You are waiting for that all-important phone call. You are John Travolta in *Saturday Night Fever.* You are pacing up and down to music. Suddenly the phone rings, the music is blaring, you rush to turn it down.

There is the voice on the other end of the line. "May I speak to [your name]?

"This is [the name of the person you met with or your agent].

"We were very impressed with you today, and"—that fateful moment of silence—"we'd like to make you an offer."

Then you fill in the details. Like how much money you want. (Do not skimp here. You will get only what you are seeing on this screen, so go for the gold.)

What do you want out of this victory you've just had? Fill in all the details.

Allow the screen to disappear, get a good night's sleep.

You've done two vital things here: First, you've already claimed the victory by phasing for it; and second, you have addressed the higher self of the person you will meet with the next day. When they meet you and you shake their hand, they won't know why, but they will feel as if they already know you. They will be open wide for you to show them your stuff!!!

P.S. If, when you get the call, you have only a couple of hours to get ready for your follow-up, choose what you will wear, hop into the shower, and phase while the water is running.

If you are called to a last-minute meeting with the boss, phase as you walk down the hall. If you have time, duck into the rest room, close the door, and phase. The point is, do not ever take an important meeting without phasing first.

You snooze, you lose. Don't forget it!!!

Ease on, Ease on Down the Road

First I was afraid, I was petrified
Thinking I could never live without you by my side
And I spent so many nights thinking how you did me wrong
But I grew strong, I learned how to get along

From "I Will Survive,"
sung by Gloria Gaynor
Words and music by Freddie Perren and Dino Fekaris

We're going to "get down to it" in this phase, and heal old relationships from our past. We are going to wipe the slate clean. By moving "in between" worlds we will heal the scars of our emotional past and move into the now and the future, free . . . free to trust again, free to love again, free to live again.

Put on your music. Allow yourself to sit comfortably erect. Place your hands on your knees, palms up. Let out all of your breath. Take a deep breath in through your nose, hold it to the count of seven, then forcefully blow the breath out of your mouth. Do this to the count of seven. Allow yourself to slip into phasing, as you review those past relationships you want to heal.

See the giant screen in front of you. Allow yourself to be aware of the emotions that are running through you. Whatever you are feeling at this moment, just let it happen. Be aware of the movement of your body as it responds to your breath.

As you take another breath, someone from your past appears on the screen. Because of the amount of pain you once felt, the amount of emotional damage you sustained, you could not allow yourself to forgive this person. I want you to see them as larger than life on that giant screen in front of you.

As you look at this person, stored-up emotions boil to the surface. All the stored anger from the past, all of the pain from your involvement with this person, is here in this moment. Your nerve endings are alive as you allow the memories of your time with this person to emerge. Don't block the emotions coming up right now. Allow yourself to have this experience of feeling all the stored-up pain, anger, and rage.

Put yourself on that giant screen with this person now. See yourself at that most vulnerable moment. A time you were most involved with this person. I want you to experience at this moment all that you did then; experience it right now!

Re-create on the giant screen the most painful encounter you experienced with the person you are now seeing. Relive it in every small detail. Feel it like you would a movie, when all of your emotions become tied to the characters on that screen, and you become them. Experience it with all you have stored inside. Take as long as you need. Just go with it!!!

Now tell that person how you really feel about your relationship with them. Make it clear to them. Tell them about all the pain and disappointment you felt. Let them see the anger and the frustration you were too afraid to reveal—because if you did, they would leave you and you would not survive. Communicate every bit of emotion you have stored up. Every single thought or feeling you were too frightened to face by yourself back then is now here, right on the tip of your tongue. Let it rip!!!

Good Work!!!

See yourself standing on the screen. You've just revealed your greatest truth to this person you once felt so attached to—this person whom you didn't think you could live without.

What is their response to you? Listen and observe with your heart.

See them for who they truly are—not the imaginary person you have built them up to be in your mind, or your expectation of who they should be for you. See the reality of them. Allow yourself to know this truth, now, this moment.

When you see them in truth, you see that all of their inadequacies, all of the little kinks in their armor, are revealed. Standing in front of you is the real person inside that person you created in your mind. Now, as you see them as they truly are, you see your part in the creation of someone who could never be. Let them go!!! Forgive, forget, and move on!!!

Repeat this phase for every hurtful relationship you've had in your life until you feel completely healed, completely free. Then do something loving for yourself. You've earned it!!!

Every time I watch the movie *The Way We Were,* I get out my box of Kleenex. There's Barbra, so passionate about her beliefs. There's Robert Redford, searching for some meaning to the charmed life he's lived. As they come together, the love between them fills the screen with a surreal glow. Then it gets complicated. As much as they love each other, they are as different as the worlds they come from.

In the last scene of the movie, there stands Robert, many years older, but still as handsome, with a beautiful girl on his arm. He looks across the street and sees Barbra handing out political fliers. He rushes across the busy New York street, looks at her, and says, "You never give up, do you?"

She answers, "Only when I'm forced to."

The look they exchange clearly shows the love that still exists between them. Barbra tells him about their daughter, now grown—a daughter he has never seen. She invites him for dinner. He looks at her and says, "I can't."

She answers, "I know."

What neither says, but the camera reveals by the expression on their faces, is that—even though they love each other—they live in different worlds.

The camera pans as Barbra goes about the business of living her life and Robert goes on about his. They have let go.

Like Barbra and Robert's characters, you, too, can love and forgive someone, but because it won't work out, you will be able to let them go.

As I am sitting here writing this, tears are streaming down my face. I am reminded of the words *Healer, heal thyself* and how this phase came to me. It was out of my own pain, out of my own inability to forgive and heal, that I asked Spirit to give me a powerful phasing experience. Before that painful experience in my own life, when I was teaching the Intraphase workshops, I thought it was enough to just guide people to their soul mates. However, from personal experience I learned that was not enough. Indeed, the scars of the past must be healed before we can attract a life mate to us. I'd like to share my story with you.

There was a man in my past. He is a beautiful man. Oh, how I loved him. Obsessively, you might say. I met him in Hawaii. The night I walked into the club where he was playing onstage, I did a double take. Several years before in meditation I had seen the face of a man. His dark eyes looked right into my soul. When I looked into this man's eyes, I relived that vision. He was everything I thought I wanted. Dark, good looks, blazing intensity, a Scorpio, and—most of all—he was a musician.

A few months before I met him, I asked Spirit to send me a lover and a soul mate. (Unbeknownst to me at the time, and contrary to popular opinion, soul mates are rarely life mates. Believe me, I learned this the hard way!)

Mind you, I did not ask Spirit for a life mate, I asked for a lover, a soul mate. (I have since learned that soul mates are people we have traveled with before, in other incarnations. Though great passion exists between soul mates, rarely is it more than that.)

A soul mate is what this man was, and passion is what we shared together. He was all of the things I'd asked for and, through no fault of his own, none of the things I didn't think to consider. So in Hawaii we became lovers. And it was the most beautiful time of my life. I'll never forget the time spent there with him. Every time I smell tuberose, I am reminded of that beautiful time, of the love and passion we shared.

The intensity between us grew. It was no longer enough for me to simply see him once in a while. I wanted him in my life here, a life that was filled with demands. My practice, my clients, my children. I had a full plate. Those of you who have built your lives around being needed will relate. These responsibilities filled an enormous part of my life, but it didn't fill the personal void inside of me. I felt so needy, I wanted him here in my life; a life he knew very little about. It wasn't that I tried to keep it from him, it was that when I spent time with him in magical Hawaii, I didn't want to think of the "real world" back home.

Somewhere deep inside of me, I knew his move to Malibu would be wrong. But I ignored the voice of Spirit and dug my heels in, determined to have it my way. So the Scorpio part of me (I have five planets in that sign) said, "Screw you, Universe, I love him and I want him in my life and I will make it work."

He moved to Malibu to be with me. I will never forget boarding the plane with him to come home; I had a knot in my stomach the size of the population of New York City. I ignored all the panic buttons flashing inside myself. Frankly, I was in denial. I just shut up that voice, shook my head, and dismissed the feelings inside, determined to make our relationship work.

Let me say: Never, ever ignore the voice of Spirit when it speaks to you. You will live to regret it!!

The move was a disaster. From day one it was a disaster for both of us. The world I lived in, the world that demanded so much of me, was a world he did not understand. It was so hard on both of us. I could not, would not, give up my practice. And unlike my fantasies in Hawaii, where I saw him giving back to me, he could not. Not in the way I desperately needed. Within six months I was totally drained. I was fighting to fill his needs, those of my clients, my children—everyone but myself. Needless to say, the pressures were horrific. My health suffered greatly.

He said he wanted to pursue his musical career (which he never did when he was with me); hence, the whole burden of the relationship fell on my shoulders. I had set it up that way. I thought I could do it. I sometimes cried in silence, begging the Universe to give me the strength to take it all on.

The breaking point came when I told him he would have to find some employment. I could no longer withstand the pressures. He was angry because the world he had lived in with me until now was shattered; I was angry because he wasn't the man I had built him up to be in my mind.

We went our separate ways. Do I love him still? Yes, of course I do. I don't think anyone who has had an experience this intense ever stops loving that person.

For the longest time I held on to the anger, the pain. Through the phasing we have just completed together, I was able to heal. I was able to let it all go, let him go.

As I look back on the whole experience, I realize he never could hear my music and I could not dance his dance.

This was my fifth telephone session with Lenita in the past six months. "Dawnea, I still haven't met the man you predicted. Where is he?"

"Lenita, let me ask you something. Are you still seeing Russell?"

I hear nothing but silence on the other end of the phone. "Lenita?"

Then a quiet little "Yes."

"Lenita, how long have you been seeing Russell?"

"Eight years."

In this work it's so hard to watch as people continually abuse themselves. When I see it, my heart aches for them, and, damn it, I get mad. I shot back at her, "Eight years? Eight years of him cheating on you, lying to you, and abusing you? And you are still with this fool? Are you crazy or do you just love the drama?"

"I know. I know what you told me, Dawnea, but I'm afraid to leave him, I'm afraid to be alone."

"Lenita, are you not alone now? The guy is seldom around, and when he is you are terrified that at any moment he's going to walk out that door. Come on, girl, how do you expect to meet a new man when you haven't owned the stored-up pain and anger over this one? Right now, as it stands, if you do meet someone new, he will be just like this guy. You've got to face all of your pain over Russell, heal it, and allow yourself to feel your own power again. When was the last time you really felt connected to yourself?"

Her quiet little voice answered, "Oh, about eight and a half years ago."

I silently shook my head in confirmation as I told her, "I rest my case. Lenita, when you let Russell and his abusive butt go; when you can stand up for yourself; when you claim your power back; that is when the 'new' man will come into your life. Not until. Come on, everything else I predicted for you has happened, right?"

"Yes, even the job change—all of it has happened."

"Well, why do you think the man isn't here?"

"Because I've got to get back to me."

"That's right, Lenita. Make that journey. Not for some great guy who's out there waiting for you—make the journey for yourself. Do you still have the phasing tape I made for you?"

"Yeah . . . I still got it."

"But you're not using it, are you?"

"Well, no. It brought up too much for me."

"That is the point. Bring it up so you can heal it."

"Okay, okay, Dawnea, I'll do it."

"Good. And Lenita?"

"Yeah?"

"Do it for you."

* * *

I received a telephone call from Lenita several months later. She used the phasing tape, worked on herself, and thus manifested the courage to leave her old boyfriend. She met the man I had been predicting for her during our first telephone session.

Yeeaaah!!! I love it when people claim back their power. How about you? Can you stand that much happiness?

"Dawnea, I cannot believe I allowed myself to be roped into Stephanie's bullshit again. How many times is she going to play these games with me?" Timothy sat with his long legs crossed. His crystal-blue eyes were covered by his long jet-black hair that tumbled down his face. He had a three-day stubble on his face.

"Timothy, honey, sorry to say this, but as long as you allow her back into your life, as long as you believe what you know to be her 'bullshit,' she will keep dumping her doo-doo on your head. What's it going to take?"

He wiped his disheveled wavy locks out of his perfect face (I'm not supposed to notice these things when I'm working but, hey, I'm human and Timothy is gorgeous and he is a musician—my weak spot. But, alas, I never cross those boundaries. Damn!)

"I know. The last time I was here I swore I would not call her, and if she called me, I wouldn't return the call."

"Timmy, did you do what I told you?"

"What?"

"Change your number?"

He whined, saying, "Then Steph couldn't get ahold of me. . . ." He looked at me right as he finished that sentence. My eyebrows were raised in frustration.

"Ah, come on, D, I'm hurtin' here."

"Your choice. And there is no point to this session. Why are you here today? Obviously, you are not ready to let her go."

"But I have to. I'm in the studio. It's fucking up my chops. She's fucking up my chops."

I stood up from my chair, walked over to him, and shouted, "No! *You* are fucking up your chops. *You* are allowing yourself to be sucked in. Get the hell out of here until you are ready to make some changes. Otherwise, you are here for nothing."

He looked at me in shock. Rarely do I raise my voice. Never do I lose my temper. Actually, I hadn't really lost my temper; I just wanted to get his attention.

Timothy smiled that million-dollar smile of his. "Ah, come on, D, make me feel better, tell me it's going to be okay."

"Timmy, it will be okay when you are ready for it to be. In the meantime, knock yourself out. Take all the shit she's dishing. When you're ready, come back in. We'll do some phasing and we will exorcise that demon from your life. Hallelujah!!"

He looked at me in shock.

I smiled. "Just kidding—my evangelical background slipping through. But I am serious about the phasing part. You are not ready yet. You haven't suffered enough." I got up, hugged him, and ushered him out of my office. All the while he was sputtering, "But—but, D . . . hey!?"

Until someone is ready to let it go, nothing will work. Not one thing will make Timothy or you change your life until you say you are ready. Nothing and no one can keep you stuck in your shit but you.

Three weeks to the day I received a phone call from Timothy. He was ready. I could tell by the tone of his voice something had made him hit the wall. Of course, I knew that something was Stephanie, but I wouldn't let him say anything over the phone. I figured I'd make him think he could tell me his horror story in the office. But I had other plans for him; he was ready to do this phase. He was ready to let her go. About time. We'd been hashing this very bad movie over for the last three years.

I greeted him at the door. He rushed past me, making a beeline for my office, anxious to get started. "Dawnea, you will not believe what happ—"

I cut him off in midsentence. "Timothy, I could tell by your voice on the phone this is the last straw. Now, I am going to ask you, are you ready to let Stephanie go?"

He nodded his head, resolve in his voice, as he said, "Hell, yes, I am ready."

"Good, let's get to work."

"But, D, I want to tell you—"

I held up my hand and stated, "No, Timmy, we're going to phase today. You are going to relive frame by frame the final breaking point, then you are going to say good-bye to Stephanie. Good-bye, once and for all. You are going to get your power back. And it's not because they are pressuring you to finish the album." (He looked at me in astonishment. He hadn't told me that.)

"As I was saying, you are going to get your power back because you are ready. You are going to start living your life. Ready?"

"Yeah."

"Good, close your eyes, relax, be aware of the room around you, the music playing in the background."

"You mean Muzak?"

"Uh, come on, Timothy, this is not the time to play Nirvana. Take a deep breath, let it go, and focus your attention on the sound of my voice, the words I am speaking. Your mind, your emotions, will do the rest. Now, breathe in through your nose and out through your mouth." I took Timmy through the circular breathing to the giant screen in his mind.

"Timmy, see Stephanie on the screen. See the breaking point. Tell me what you are seeing. Just get it all out."

"Well, I got out of the studio around six in the morning. We'd pulled an all-nighter, things just weren't clicking.

"Anyway, I stopped at the all-night market and bought some stuff to make Steph breakfast. I thought I would surprise her. Things had been so cool the last few days. Anyway, I get to her place, I unlock the door, take the stuff to the kitchen. I saunter into her bedroom, taking my clothes off as I go, and what do I find?

"She's in bed with another man. Not just another man, but Ren, the lead singer of the band I fucking hate. Why do I hate them? Because they have no talent. And because he rips my shit every time he can in public."

I flinched as I relived that moment with him. "Timmy, what did you do?"

His voice got deathly calm as he told me, "I saw her for who she was: a white-trash opportunity seeker; not the love of my life. Then I started laughing. Man, I laughed my ass off. I looked at Ren and said, 'Knock yourself out, man, just don't catch anything.' "

"Did you say anything to Stephanie?"

He laughed, saying, "Yeah, I said, 'I left you some eggs.' I walked out of the house and never looked back."

"Timmy, how do you feel right now watching yourself reliving that moment?"

"Cured. Man, I love this phasing. It's like watching a movie of your life. Right on!"

Timothy called me the next week. As usual, he left a long message on my service when he couldn't reach me. I'll just sum it up. It worked.

Patricia sat in the chair across from me. She was a stunning woman in her late forties, her hair cut blunt around a face that showed not one wrinkle (damn it!). Her perfectly toned body was clothed in Armani, her bag Gucci. Everything about her spoke of money and affluence. Everything, that is, except her gray eyes, which were spilling over with her pain. When I ushered her into my office, I could feel that pain. It wafted off her in waves. To the regular eye she was perfection and control, but to my eye this woman was clearly suffering.

She sat in the chair, hands folded neatly, staring at me, waiting for she wasn't sure what.

"Patricia, I can feel your suffering. I would like to work with you today in a different kind of session. I'd like to phase with you. Someone has torn your heart out."

She raised her perfectly arched eyebrow.

"Yes, I'm going through a divorce."

"Do you know what your husband has been up to? Have you protected yourself? After all you gave this man—what? Twenty-plus years?"

Again surprised registered on her face at my intuitive comment. "Twenty-one years six months, to be exact." Patricia fought gallantly to control her pent-up emotions.

"Patricia, I know you came to hear about your future today, and you do have one, believe me—there is another man for your life. I saw him this morning in meditation. But before he can come in, you've got to heal the scars your husband has embedded in your heart.

"Will you trust me? I feel this is the fastest way we can heal those open wounds you are carrying inside."

She let out a ragged breath and said, "Anything. I just want to get on with my life."

"That's the spirit. Close your eyes, take a deep breath in through your nose, hold it, let it out through your mouth." I took Patricia through the circular breathing to the giant screen in her mind.

"Patricia, I want you to surf through those painful memories in your soul and see yourself on that giant screen. See the you who just found out all about her husband. The husband you thought you knew is gone. This new stranger stands in front of you. What do you want to do? What do you want to say to him?"

She did not miss a beat as years of repressed anger spewed out of her. "Douglas, I hate you. I hate you for lying to me for all of these years. I hate your lies. You lied about money, you lied about women, you lied about everything. And the sick thing is, everyone around us knew but me." Patricia stopped for a moment, then she let out this ironic little laugh and continued. "Yes, even our closest friends knew you were a liar."

I urged her on. "You're doing great! Get it all out, tell him how you feel."

"You know what I'm going to do, Douglas? I'm going to hire a detective. I am going to find out just how badly you have been cheating me all these years. Yes, me— sweet, innocent, pathetically trusting Patricia. I do have a brain. I plan to take you by surprise, my dear. You think I'm going to just stand by and watch you walk away with it all? No, my dear Douglas, I plan to extract your balls."

Hey, now we were getting somewhere.

"Patricia, I want you to tell Douglas how you felt

about all the years you gave to him. Tell him everything."

"You always made me feel like I was second best. Like you were the star and I was the little faithful shadow behind you, to be there for your every need. But what about my needs . . . ?" Her voice broke then, the tears finally came rushing out of her. Bless her heart. After years of stored-up pain and rejection the dam was breaking. She gulped for breath and went on. "In the last ten years you never once told me I was beautiful or that you appreciated all I did. All the dinner parties for your boring egotistical colleagues. All of the effort to make you look good with my charity work, raising the children by myself because you were too damn busy. You were on location, you were worried about the money, you were in a meeting. Too many late meetings, too many trips away, too much of you and nothing left for me. I've had it. I'm glad it's over. I am beautiful and I am not too old to love and to be loved. Goddamn it, I'm going to start spending some of the money I helped you to earn. Good-bye, Douglas, I'll see you in court."

I couldn't have put it better myself. Patricia opened her eyes, a look of determination on her face.

"Patricia, I'm proud of you. What a session!"

"You know something, Dawnea? I saw more than I said. I must have some of your gift or it rubbed off on me. That man has been cheating me for years. I meant what I said, I'm taking my life back. Then I know I will meet someone. I don't need to hear it today. I have work to do."

*   *   *

Patricia did meet her life mate, and you'll read about him in "Phase Six—The Sequel." She also hired the detective and she took *real* good care of herself. Her husband had no idea how smart she was. His loss!

All of these brave people worked hard to clear the anger and pain of their past relationships. And by doing so they were able to move ahead into the future, to trust again, to love again—and so will you.

When you find your life mate, you will fit. Just like the pieces of a puzzle, your lives will blend together. Oh, don't worry, there will be plenty of love and passion as well. Which brings me to . . . "Phase Six—The Sequel."

When Love Comes to Town

A long time ago
I made up my mind
I'm saving myself 'cause someday I'll find
Someone like you
Waiting for someone like me

From the song "Let's Make the First Time Last"
Words by Gloria Sklerov, Robin Tapp,
and John Boegehold

Get ready! You are going to meet your life mate. This is the phase where you lock in to that person, that other half of yourself. Not only will you see them, you will feel them in your heart.

In the last phase you healed the scars from old relationships. In doing that you opened a space inside your heart to attract love—the real kind of unconditional love—into your life.

Why put off finishing what we started?

Lights, camera, action, let's get to work!!!

* * *

Set the ambience for this one. Light some candles and some incense. Or spray some of your favorite cologne around the room, preferably the scent you would find most appealing on your lover. (But not a lover from your past!!!)

Put on some soft, sensuous music. This is where Suzanne Ciani's song "The Velocity of Love" really works.

Sit comfortably and complete your circular breathing. See the giant screen in front of you. Anticipation is building. Let it. Suzanne or your favorite "love" music is playing in the background, the candlelight is flickering, you smell the sensuous aroma in the air.

The outer scene is set so your senses can experience the powerful sensations going on inside you—the you that is phasing.

A beautiful mountaintop appears on the giant screen. It's filled with wildflowers of every color imaginable. The blue sky has tiny puffy white clouds that skirt past as the gentle wind blows them onward.

You see yourself lying under an ancient oak tree with gnarled branches that reach far into the blue sky. You touch the bark of the tree, feeling its texture, its life, its wisdom. This tree has lived long enough to see many come and go. In this moment you grasp the connection between you, the tree, the warm earth beneath you. You inhale the fragrant beauty of the flowers that surround you. Your mind reaches up to the blue sky above. You are at peace, total peace, with all that is here. Allow yourself to absorb this moment as you watch it on the screen.

From a distance you feel someone approaching. You sit up, shade your eyes to see who it is. At first you see no one, merely feel him. (Of course, for some of you it will be a her.) You sit watching curiously, your eyes searching in the direction you feel that someone to be.

A tiny speck of a figure appears on the horizon. Your heart starts beating faster. There is something . . . something so familiar about this scene. As though you have lived it before.

The tiny speck becomes a person. Footsteps tread lightly on the flowered field as he approaches you. You cannot see his face, but you know he is smiling. Joy and anticipation spring into your heart as you not only watch, but feel, this scene take on life.

As if an eternity has passed, finally he is close enough for you to make out his features. Not the face, but what he is wearing, how tall he is, the shape of his body. You stand, leaning back against the ancient oak, waiting—and knowing—that it is for you that he has come to this place.

Finally, he is near you. Look at his face. His features are clear to you now: the color of his hair, his eyes, the shape of his mouth. All of it. See him in complete detail.

As the you on the screen is observing him, so is the you that is sitting, watching this whole scene.

You and your life mate are standing face-to-face. Gently, softly, he takes your hands, holding them in his. Feel how you respond to his touch.

You look into each other's eyes. How familiar they are; it's as though you have been looking into those eyes lifetime after lifetime. Oh, you know this person so well. Everything about him is familiar. A rush of excitement washes over you.

You tenderly lie down together under the ancient tree. Your hearts, your souls, your bodies, your emotions, merge. You become one heart, one soul, one mind.

Allow yourself to savor this moment; you've waited a lifetime for this exact time and place. Let the emotions that you are feeling bond you deeply to this picture on the screen in your mind.

Make it real with all you have. Do it now!!!

Now take this one step farther. On the giant screen in your mind, allow the movie to play on. See yourself with this person in your day-to-day life. See the two of you sharing all that is your world, the world of the now, where—from this moment on— you are no longer alone. You are sharing the world you now live in and the world you will create together.

Allow the screen in your mind to disappear. You have meshed your entire being with what you've just experienced. There is nothing standing in the way for this to manifest in your life. So be it!!!

I loved that movie *French Kiss.* It starts with Meg Ryan inside a simulated airplane. You hear a voice say, "Kate, what are you seeing?"

With anxiety etched on her face Meg (Kate) answers tersely, "Broken bodies, twisted steel, a naked baby screaming for its mother."

The calm voice, coming over the intercom, says, "Kate, where's your little stone cottage on the hill? Picture it now."

The movie plays on. Her fiancé flies to France, falls in love with a French girl, and Kate goes after him. In doing so she meets her life mate (played by Kevin Kline)—though, for the better part of the movie, to each other they seem an unlikely pair. As the movie progresses, I'm there cheering them on. It's obvious they are meant to be together. Which is, of course, exactly what happens.

Cut to the last scene of the movie: Meg and Kevin, hand-in-hand, walking through a vineyard next to Kate's (Meg's) little stone cottage. (The one she had "phased" to overcome her fear of flying.)

Ah, phasing, it's a powerful thing. Yes, your intuition and your mind, connected to your emotions, are a powerful thing indeed.

Carla sat in the relationship phasing workshop, brow furrowed, taking furious notes. I had the group close their eyes. We began phasing. I took the group on a journey similar to the one you have just taken. They were to meet their life mates.

When I finished leading the room through the movie in their minds, I glanced at Carla. Her cheeks were flushed, her eyes filled with tears.

The evening was over, people were milling around, sharing their experiences. Carla was waiting patiently to speak to me.

"Carla, did you get what you needed tonight?"

Her eyes were glowing. "You know, Dawnea, I've taken so many classes, spent so much money on workshops, but tonight—with the movie in my mind—the way you described it, I actually felt—not just saw but felt—my life mate. It was so powerful."

I hugged her small frame and said, "I'm so happy for you. Carla? Stay with that feeling. Keep it locked inside."

She smiled, then turned and walked out of the room with a few others.

Two years passed before I received a telephone call from Carla. She wanted to book a joint session with me. Truthfully, at the time she called, I had forgotten who she was.

When she arrived for her session, that evening long since past came back to me. By then I had stopped doing workshops and was concentrating on intensive one-on-one sessions with my clients. It was so rewarding to remember how deeply that evening had touched her and others. I was so lost in those memories, I forgot there was someone with her.

I winked at Carla and said, "Let me guess—the result of the workshop?"

She beamed. "Yes, right down to the shape of his hands."

I laughed. "Just goes to show you how powerful phasing can be."

I extended my hand to the man with Carla. "I'm Dawnea. I didn't mean to leave you out. Do you even know what phasing is?"

He laughed. In a slight drawl he said, "The name's Derek and, oh, yeah, I know all about phasing. I've been hearing about it for months."

Derek was a lovely man—dark hair, large, expressive green eyes. I could feel his energy. He had a warm, loving heart. I was so happy for Carla, and I had to agree—he had great hands.

I welcomed them both, took a deep breath, and went to work.

Terrence sat across from me, holding Eric's hand. He was beaming. Eric looked more than a little nervous.

"Eric, did Terrence drag you here today?"

He hesitated.

"It's okay. I'm used to people being nervous around me. It's nothing. By the end of this session I guarantee you'll be fine. Just fine."

He looked at me, skepticism written all over his face. I smiled to myself, and said, " 'The proof's in the puddin',' as my daddy used to say."

I looked from Eric to Terrence and commented, "I know you are not the same young man who sat in this very office six months ago, crying over that sorry fool Tony."

He looked from Eric, back to me, then back again. "No, I am not that same young man, Dawnea. The session we did in your treatment room opened my eyes to so many things."

A clear picture formed in my mind: Terrence lying there on the table, tears sliding down his cheeks, as the screen in his mind revealed that awkward adolescent boy who was so angry at him. That little boy who was so ashamed of who he really was. That little boy who was terrified his famous athlete father would find out he was gay.

My mind came back to the present and I asked, "Terrence, tell me what's been goin' on."

"You know, D, I finally got it. All the relationships I'd had up to now were with men who validated the very thing my father did."

I knew what he meant. We had "phased" it out when he was in my office last. His father did find out Terrence was gay—his sister told him. He had not spoken to or acknowledged Terrence since. That was fifteen years ago. Since then Terrence had had a string of abusive relationships. It tore at my heart to think about it.

I cast an intuitive look at Eric while I was speaking to Terrence.

"What did that session do for you, Terrence?"

"To tell you the truth, the whole scene put me out of my mind. I was so blown away when I left your office. But I think the thing that turned it around for me was seeing and feeling the man who was my life mate. This man"—he squeezed Eric's hand—"this gorgeous man sitting right here."

I had to agree with Terrence. Eric was stunning.

I laughingly said, "Damn, boyfriend, I need to hone up on my manifesting skills—Terrence is right. Eric, you are fine. . . ."

Eric laughed out loud. I could tell he was finally allowing himself to relax.

There were some bridges to cross in the session I did for the boys that day. They were life mates. But both had come from wounded backgrounds. Both had issues about trust. We talked those and other issues out. By the end of the hour Eric was really letting go. I looked at him and said, "Looks like you're over your paranoia about intuitives, huh?"

He just smiled.

Terrence shot him a sassy little look and said, "I told you she was cool, man."

Eric laughed. "Yeah, she's way cool. And she'd be even cooler if she'd let us use her steps to the beach."

I hugged them both, opened my office door to the backyard and the steps beyond, and invited, "Be my guest. You both worked hard today, you've earned a walk on the beach."

Patricia sat across from me, clearly a different woman. Her eyes were radiant, she'd let her hair grow down to her shoulders. She still dressed impeccably, but she now had a new sassiness about her.

"Patricia, you look fantastic."

"And I feel it. I don't want to waste any time. Can we get started?"

"Okay, let's do it." I took a deep breath; I was excited for Patricia. "Start your circular breathing . . . now see the giant screen in your mind." Patricia went on the journey to meet her life mate. As he was approaching her, I could see that he was the man I had seen in meditation several months before. Only, he was better than I'd seen. Oh, I love this work!!!

When she was through phasing, Patricia opened her tear-filled eyes and said, "Dawnea, I saw him."

Smiling back, I said, "Yeah, what did he look like?"

She laughed. "You know. I know you saw him too."

"I did, but I want you to tell me about him."

"Well"—she blushed and stumbled on—"He's, um . . . younger, younger than me."

"Uh-huh, and?"

"You don't think that's bad?"

"Are you kidding? My dear, it is not age that matters, not one iota. Why is it that women think it's not okay to be with a younger man but men do it all the time?"

She laughed, saying, "You mean like Douglas?"

I shot back, "Isn't he going to be pissed when he finds out? Oh, this is too much fun!"

Patricia was beaming from ear to ear as she continued. "Back to the man. He is younger and attractive, he has the most beautiful golden eyes I've ever seen. He's a little taller than me." (Patricia is five eight.)

"He's funny, he's sexy, and we have a business together. He's in film. He and I work together."

Listening to Patricia now, I had to smile. See how far you can go in these phasing sessions?

"Well, you know I've started working again. My women friends really supported me through this nightmare. Jeri offered me a job at her production company, and I love it. I feel so alive again. Anyway, this man and I are going to work together, travel together, and we are going to love together. I can't wait. How long do you think it will take to 'bring him in'?"

"The more you work with this phasing session, the sooner it will happen."

"Then I'm taking this tape wherever I go. I want it now. I've wasted enough time. I don't want to waste another minute."

Didn't take long. Patricia met Chad six months later. I performed their wedding ceremony.

What about me in this phase? I haven't met my life mate yet. Why? Because I haven't phased for it. I haven't been ready either; I've been too busy writing!

Yakety-Yak, Please Talk Back

I know you think you heard what I said, but did you hear what I meant? Did you listen with your heart? Or did you listen with your pride?

The Intraphase Workshops, 1987

One of the most common causes of misunderstanding in relationships—all types of relationships—is lack of communication. Phase Seven will help you achieve a level of communication you never knew was possible, teaching you how to verbalize what it is you truly want to say to those around you—and how to listen not with your ego but with your heart.

Put on some music, sit comfortably erect, blow out all of your breath through your mouth. Complete your circular breathing and begin phasing. See the giant screen in front of you. On that screen see a person in your life whom you want to communicate with better than you've been able to because you're afraid to speak the truth or they're unable to hear it.

Observe the person on the screen for a moment; study their

body language. Ask yourself if it suggests someone who is open to you, or closed off.

Once you have gotten a read of the situation, place yourself up there on the giant screen alongside the person you want to communicate with.

Gently, leading with your heart, ask what you can do to create open communication between the two of you.

Watch and listen, as the person on the screen opens up and responds, telling you the feelings you've been unable to talk about. Be aware of yourself as you sit there, watching the communication taking place on the screen. How are you feeling? Do you feel open as you watch and listen? Are you angry? If so, ask the you on the screen to convey to that person that you are angry and why. Then watch and listen as that person responds to your anger.

Remind yourself that you are in a totally safe place—a place of love where you can speak directly from the heart. Watch and listen as the you on the screen tells the person up there exactly how you feel.

Keep paying close attention to how you feel as you sit there and watch. Is your anger going away? Continue to share your feelings while the movie you talks it all out with the person up there. The two of you will communicate until you have reached one another.

If the communication is complete, you will feel a powerful breakthrough.

You have listened and you have been heard.

Allow the screen in front of you to disappear. Go over the conversation you have just had with that person on the screen.

*   *   *

Next move: Put what you have just phased into motion.

Take a deep breath, recall the "love space" you shared when you were communicating with the person on the screen. Now call them with an open heart—they will feel the difference—and ask them to lunch or for coffee. When you get together, you'll notice that things feel different, because you have opened a door and addressed that person's "higher mind," the part of all of us that is not motivated by ego or fear.

If you do not feel ready to face the person (it's okay, you're human), sit down and write a letter. Write all of your feelings out.

If there was a certain incident that was the "breaking point," put it in words. Hold on to the letter for seven days, then go back and reread it. If the words you wrote still feel like they are your truth, put a stamp on the letter, give it a kiss, and mail it.

"And they lived happily ever after." . . . Not!!!

Relationships, if they are to last, take a lot of work. The most important thing for you, as a life mate, to be aware of is: communication. Not only physical communication, but verbal as well. These two areas of communication are the foundation of your life together. If your mate says something to you that is hurtful, or angers you, do not hold it inside. Do not allow it to fester. When it hurts, say so—"Ouch, baby, that hurt"—and say it as soon as it happens.

The moment either of you feels the communication breaking down, it's time to phase together.

Set aside quality time alone; if you have to get a baby-sitter, do so. Do not allow these things to build up. When you allow them to build up, they tend to have the dynamite effect: They blow up!!!

Sit facing one another, fingertips touching. Look each other in the eye. Say aloud to one another, "I love you." Feel the electricity that passes between your fingertips. Once you have established a rapport, communicate—get down, get funky. Let each other know how the other feels. Get it all out. You will know when you've reached a point of healing. You will feel it. And until you feel the complete healing, do not have sex.

Many couples use sex as a way to avoid dealing with verbal communication. Nothing gets accomplished. Okay, maybe you have a great orgasm, but that still doesn't solve the lack of verbal communication. After the sex is over, the emotional wedge will still be there, and more often than not the resentment will be stronger.

So . . . you get to "get down" *after* you have healed each other emotionally. I guarantee you the sex will be awesome. Not only will you be bonding physically, you will be bonding emotionally and spiritually. It will blow your mind!!! (Not to mention various body parts!)

When Harry Met Sally is one of my favorite Meg Ryan films. (Okay, Billy, you are hilarious in the movie too.) I am amazed at how the script captures the way all of us often *do* and *do not* communicate what we *really* think or feel.

The film begins with Harry and Sally fresh out of college driving cross-country to begin their new lives in New York. On the trip they both agree how different they are and that they cannot see eye-to-eye on anything.

They arrive in New York, shake hands, and go their separate ways. However, fate has other plans for them. Good old fate throws them together, first as friends, then—one night—as lovers. Everything in their friendship changes after that night. Harry becomes distant, Sally is hurt. (How familiar does that sound?) Finally, it's New Year's Eve. Sally is with her friends at a party. She is alone and it is obvious to us, the viewing audience, she does not want to be there. Harry is alone in his apartment, thinking about Sally. He decides to take a walk on the empty streets of New York, trying desperately to convince himself he's okay, but his mind keeps playing the memories of Sally. It is near midnight, he can't stand it anymore. He breaks into a dead run. He reaches the party just before the stroke of twelve. Sally sees him and tries to ignore that he is there. Harry insists they go outside. Sally tells him she will not be his consolation prize. He looks at her and, hallelujah, he finally tells her how he really feels about her.

In life, when you are clear about the fact that you can communicate your true feelings, that you will be heard because you will make yourself heard, you, too, can have the yummy cake with the sauce on the side. Do it! Tell it!! Just talk it out!!!

Hope and Phil sat together on the wicker love-seat. Both of them had their arms crossed tightly against their chests. Both of their faces were filled with anger and frustration.

"Okay, guys, let's go to work. Who wants to start?"

Hope answered, "Dawnea, every time I try to tell Phil how I feel, he gets so angry he grabs his car keys, stomps out of the house, and drives off."

Phil, face bright red, spits out, "That's bullshit, Hope. You nag and nag and push my buttons, until I can't take it. So, instead of breaking something, I get the hell out."

Hope retorts, "Well, if you would listen to what I say when I say it, instead of sticking your nose in the television, we might have a better relationship."

Exasperated, Phil raises his hands in the air and says, "Oh, that's right, I'm the asshole. You—Saint Hope—are never wrong, are you?"

After that outburst they both sat with their arms and legs crossed, seething. I let them sit there and stew.

After a while I took a deep breath, drawing them both in as I said, "You've heard that Dave Mason song 'We Just Disagree,' haven't you? You know, no bad guys or good guys—just the two of you."

They laughed a little, nodding their heads in agreement.

"So, what's going on here is both of you are so afraid

of being wrong that neither one of you is listening to the other. Oh, granted you hear, but you hear selectively. Both of you are waiting for the other one to say something or do something. Then you, Phil, can either tune out or run out. And you, Hope, are so afraid of being not heard by Phil that you do selective communicating. You feel that if you criticize him first, he won't criticize you, correct?"

They looked at each other in amazement, then back at me, vigorously nodding.

"Okay, let's do some phasing together." I took the two of them through a phasing session similar to the one about relationships I did for you.

They opened their eyes, and for the first time in that hour, they were in sync with one another.

"Guys, I have a 'miniphase' to teach you. Right now I want you to give each other a key to your defense mechanisms."

Phil asked, "What do you mean, Dawnea?"

"When you guys are in crisis mode, you don't have time to stop and touch fingertips. If you're really pissed at one another, you won't want to anyway." They laughed in agreement.

"So, what I want you to do is think of something, right now, that will get past the anger. Maybe it's a key word, or maybe it's a quick touch. Whatever—get the picture?"

Hope laughed and said, "Yeah, mine would be to say to Phil, 'Minnie Mouse.' "

Phil started laughing and added, "That's perfect."

I smiled and said, "You know what they say, laughter really is the best form of medicine." Their laughter was all the confirmation I needed.

"Good. Now, Phil, what about you?"

"Hope responds to touch, so I would touch her on the shoulder."

"Hope, does that feel right to you?"

She touched Phil's hand and said, "Yes, yes, it does."

I looked at both of them. Their arms were uncrossed. Hope's leg was across Phil's. Their hands were joined.

"You see, guys? Look at you now, compared to how you were when you first sat down." They looked at one another, squeezing their joined hands.

"The most important thing to remember is: Don't let it pile up. When something needs to be said, say it!!!"

A few months later I received a beautiful card from Hope and Phil. They were phasing and it was working. Phil was no longer running out of the house, and Hope had stopped her nagging.

Sabrina sat in my office, eyes aglow, her toes wiggling. I could see she was excited. Something had definitely shifted since our last session where we phased seeking the right course for landing the right parts.

"Sabrina, tell me what's going on."

"Our last session was so helpful to me. I went on an audition the next week. I phased on my way over there. And you know what, Dawnea? For the first time since I started going out three years ago, I felt totally in my power."

"Sabrina, that's great."

"It gets better. I didn't hear from them for three days and I really got down on myself. I was even blaming you. Saying, 'Oh, that shit's just like all the rest. It doesn't work, it's just silly words.' About the time I had thrown myself on the bed for a good cry, the phone rang.

"I let the machine pick it up until I heard who it was. It was the casting director. I got it! I got the part! I am so grateful I met you."

"Sabrina, you were ready. If you hadn't been led to me, it would have been someone else who helped you. It's your time. I have really good feelings about this."

She looked up at the ceiling and said, "From your lips to the Goddess's and the God's ears."

Not only did the film Sabrina costarred in do well, she got nominated for best supporting actress!

Allan sat across from me, anxiety written all over his face. "Dawnea, I've tried using the communication phase to help me with my boss. It's not working. I have a deadline to meet and she keeps sabotaging everything I've worked so hard to accomplish."

"Allan, have you actually confronted her? I mean, have you gone to her after your phasing and confronted her in person?"

"Well . . . no, I'm chicken. She is such a controlling bitch."

"Yes, that is partially true. I get the 'vibe' she is incredibly lonely. I also get she has no life outside of the office."

"Well, that's not my problem. I mean what do you expect me to do, date her?"

I raised my eyebrow. "No, no, that is not what I am saying. What I am saying is you have to *use* phasing in your life to make it work. Go to her, talk to her, just do it. What have you got to lose?"

Allan grinned ruefully. "Oh, only my job."

"Bullshit, Allan, you are not going to lose your job. Neither are you going one step further in that job until you confront this woman. Call me and let me know what happens."

Allan called me two days later. "Dawnea, I talked to Colleen. Two days ago I stopped in her office. I confronted her."

"How did it go?"

"She told me she wasn't trying to step on my head, she was just trying to give me suggestions. She said every time she tried to talk to me I would shrug her off. So she got pissed and decided to make my life hell."

"And you said?"

"I said I was sorry that I didn't listen, and I asked her to stop singling me out for ridicule." He laughed. "You know what she did?"

"What?"

"She held out her hand and asked, 'Truce?'

"I took her hand and answered, 'Truce.' "

"So you were *both* at fault."

"Yep, I just didn't want to see it. Actually, you know the truth? I saw it while I was phasing; there was one moment where I saw her shoulders slumped. I just thought I was making it up."

I laughed. "I thought I taught you better."

"You did. I just didn't want to listen."

"You mean you didn't want to be wrong?"

"Who does?"

"Allan, no one does, but sometimes we are, and it takes one hell of a person to admit it when they are."

Of all the challenges I face in this work, one of the hardest to cope with involves people who, for whatever reason, stay stuck in their shit when I can see so clearly where they can be in their lives.

It's as if they have "selective hearing," and hear only what they want to hear. When things don't work out, inevitably, they will blame everyone else instead of looking at the choices they made for themselves—instead of looking at the fact that they refused to listen to the truth.

Communication is the most vital component in all of your relationships. When you carry a big chip on your shoulder, when you think everyone is out to get you, as Allan did, you have selective hearing. Phase Seven can help you hear the truth—the whole truth—and help you speak your own truth in response. But as you've seen, it doesn't stop on the screen; this is one phase where it's up to you to put the healing into action.

The other choice here is to listen to the inner "Voice" that speaks to you. That voice comes from your highest good. It wants what will bring you joy in your life. Then listen with an "open ear" to others in your life. You don't have to agree with them, but if you listen, you will learn and you will grow as a person, into the beautiful soul you are meant to be.

Who Said That?

There comes a time when all of the cosmic tumblers have clicked into place and the Universe opens itself up for a few seconds to show you what is possible. . . .

From the movie *Field of Dreams*

We're all familiar with the notion of "the Voice"—a source of pure truth that speaks to those who are spiritually attuned to hear it. Past cultures believed this voice could speak only to shamans or mystics, or to individuals who have attained a level of holiness or sacred wisdom reached by a select few. In our world today we know that the same voice can speak to all who will allow themselves to listen with their inner ear and with their heart.

Today, we call that voice "intuition." You have this voice inside you, and I think it's high time we accessed it. Don't you?

* * *

Put on your music and sit comfortably. You know the drill. Do your circular breathing. Prepare to phase.

Think about a question or problem that is baffling to you. It can be related to anything: your job, relationships, children, friends, a move, a trip, or anything having to do with the day-to-day. Nothing is trivial to your intuition. It can assist you in matters both small and profound, for it already knows all about you—past, present, and future. It is the voice of your higher mind.

Take a moment to ponder the question or dilemma that you want help in. Allow the indecision to dance around your mind, to play with your emotions.

See the giant screen in your mind. See yourself on the screen sitting beside a still, glassy lake in the forest. It's sunrise, a little chilly; you are dressed warmly, having pulled your coat closely around you. You take a breath, smelling the pine needles that you are sitting on. You gaze at your own reflection in the still water. As the sun slowly rises, it reflects its beautiful dawning on the lake. Colors blend—the pink and orange in the sky with the pink and orange on the water. Water and sky are one.

You are completely at peace. Though your question or problem is presently on your mind, you are not anxious or concerned. Your senses are caught up in the beauty of your surroundings.

You hear the crunching of pine needles. Someone is approaching. The you sitting in this peaceful place opens your eyes as this person sits down next to you. *Who* is sitting next to you? Visualize in vivid detail. It may be a woman, it may be a man, it may be an angel or an extraterrestrial; whatever your first impression is, go with it. Trust it!

"Why are you here?" you ask him.

"Why? You sent for me," he answers.

You look at him, confused, knowing full well you did not send for him.

He hears your thoughts and says, "Yes, you did. You have a question about the outcome of something of importance that is taking place now in your life. Isn't that true?"

Hesitantly, you answer, "Well, yes, but—"

He chuckles a little and adds, "But nothing. Speak to me about your dilemma."

And so you do. You tell him everything about your indecision concerning your question or problem, as he listens intently to your story.

As you finish, he looks at you with love-filled eyes, and for a few moments neither you nor he says a word. You just sit there, drawing from the environment, drawing strength and healing.

He gently takes your hand and speaks. Listen carefully to what he is saying. Not only will he answer the question or the dilemma, he will also tell you what lies ahead. What the outcome will be because of the choices you are making.

You know what you are hearing, what you are experiencing, is truth. You know it because all of your emotions are responding. You are no longer in the midst of indecision. You feel at peace.

Allow the giant screen to disappear, keeping the resolution locked inside of you.

There are times when you need to make a quick decision and you are not in an environment where you can call up the giant screen in your mind's eye. At those times simply state, "Divine Order." By saying these two words you are calling on all of the forces of the Universe to assist you. Your decision will be clear to you.

Do it. It works!

How do you know whether the guidance you're hearing is the voice of your ego or the voice of your intuition? If you do not feel settled emotionally after hearing your answer, your ego is having its way.

When that happens, take a deep breath and state, "I come from pure intent."

Take a deep breath, let it go, then restate the question to your intuitive mind. Keep doing it until you feel at peace with the answer. It will come, and when it does—trust it! Act upon it!!

Field of Dreams, with Kevin Costner, is one of the most beautiful movies about intuition I have ever seen.

The movie starts with Kevin's voice describing his life up to that point, ending with the statement "Until I heard the Voice, I never done a crazy thing in my whole life."

The voice he was talking about had instructed him, "If you build it, he will come."

Kevin is prompted by that voice to plow under part of his corn crop and build a baseball field. He doesn't know why he has to do it, he just knows he does. You see the townspeople watching him, thinking, *He's lost his mind.*

He tells his young daughter the story his father had told him when he was a little boy. The story of his father's hero, "Shoeless Joe Jackson," a great ball player who was accused of "throwing" a game. He finishes the story by telling his daughter that Shoeless Joe was her granddad's hero.

One night, his little daughter looks out the window and tells him that there's a man on their grass.

Kevin looks out the window and goes outside; there, standing in his baseball field, is Shoeless Joe Jackson. In amazement, he walks onto the field where Joe is standing. Joe points; there stands Kevin's dad as a young ball player.

Kevin knew that while his father lived, he gave up his dream (his Chosen Destiny) and lived a life (his Conditioned Destiny) that aged him, well before his time. A life that caused him to die an early death.

And yet, there behind the batter's box, dressed in his uniform and catcher's equipment, is Kevin's father—the young man who was Kevin's dad, living his dream, playing ball.

He asks Kevin, "Is this heaven?"

Kevin answers, "No, this is Iowa."

Kevin turns to his father and asks, "Is there a heaven?"

"Oh, yes," he says, "it's the place where dreams come true."

*   *   *

During the short time I was living with my mother, I experienced things in a way I never had before. My mother was a triple Scorpio, and a telepath like my-self—except for her the ability was frightening. She lived in a constant state of agitation. Sometimes she would run screaming out of the house because of what she was seeing. My heart ached for her; I didn't understand why she was so afraid of her gifts. I asked her once. She looked at me with her luminescent blue eyes and said, "Because I see horrible things. I always see death."

One night when I was about thirteen years old I woke up from a sound sleep. I went out to the living room, where my mother was sitting on the couch, her back turned to me. She said, "Oh, you heard me. I was calling for you. Only, not with my voice, with my mind. Come and sit by me, I need to ask you something."

I sat down next to her. The living room was dark, with only the light from the hallway reflecting in the room, so I couldn't see very well. "Sit closer to me, honey."

I scooted next to her and looked down. She was hold-ing a gun in her hands. I held my breath and asked, "Momma, what are you doing with that?"

Her small voice answered me, "That's why I called you. If I put this up to my head, will you pull the trigger for me?"

I gasped. Tears of panic surged to my eyes. "Momma, you don't mean this. Tomorrow you will wake up and it will be okay. It's just the night. Please, Momma, give me the gun." I took a deep breath, willing whatever was tormenting her, whatever ghosts were lurking, to go away. It took the better part of an hour. I poured all the energy I could into this woman I barely knew. This woman—my mother.

Finally, I was able to get the gun away from her and she fell asleep on the couch. I covered her with a blanket and hid the gun where I thought she'd never find it.

The next morning when I woke, she was standing over me. I opened my eyes, as she sat down on the bed. "You know, I remember last night. Thank you for loving me enough to stay with me, to talk me out of shooting myself in the head. I don't know why you love me. I don't deserve it, but thank you."

She started to walk out of the bedroom, then she turned and said, "It's really how I feel, you know. I don't know why I'm down here. Some nights, I think I should just leave, go to the other side, come back another time. Maybe I wouldn't have screwed up as much as I've done in this life."

Torn between compassion and confusion (I was thirteen years old), I tried to understand, oh, how I tried.

Had it not been for my own telepathy, I would never have awakened out of my sleep. I certainly would never have had the wisdom to talk my mother out of killing herself. That wisdom did not come from a girl of thirteen, it came from outside of me. It came from "the Voice."

*   *   *

"Dawnea, I should have listened to my intuition, but I didn't. Damn, am I regretting it now! You know how it goes? The ego just kicked in and I couldn't do it. You know how it goes?"

I smiled and said, "Yes, I've been guilty of the same thing myself."

Bill's eyes widened. He looked at me as if to say, *Not you?*

"Go on, Bill, tell me what happened."

"I wanted so much for this project to work. I didn't care how I did it, I just wanted it done." Bill sat across from me, anxiety marked all over his face.

"So, Bill, where are you now with it?"

"Truth?"

I raised an eyebrow at him.

"The whole damn thing is down the tubes. When I called you a few months ago, remember?"

I nodded, waiting for him to continue.

"I knew what you were telling me was true. I just didn't want to hear it. As a matter of fact, I phased over it and got the exact answer. But, goddamn it, it would have meant giving in to Evans, and I'll be damned if I let him have the power in this project."

Bill looked at me helplessly and said, "You know, this thing is my baby. But now I'm screwed. The investors have pulled out and I am not only facing my own ruin, but my partner's as well. You know how it is in this business. People even smell any kind of failure, it's over. No one will return your phone calls, let alone touch you."

I took a deep breath, seeing in my mind's eye an entirely different outcome from the picture Bill was painting.

"Okay. Bill, do you want to phase on this or do you simply want me to tell you what I see?"

"Screw the phasing, just tell me what you see."

I frowned; the teacher within me was irritated. Should I use my telepathic gifts and put a Band-Aid on his dilemma by giving him the picture blazing across my mind, or should I make him do the work?

I glanced over at Bill. His hands were gripping the chair, his knee was wiggling up and down, his face contorted with stress.

The hell with it. I'd answer his question—partially—then make him use his own intuition to finish it.

"Okay, it's not a done deal. You can go back to that guy Evans works with. Harry. Wasn't that his name? They have recently had a falling-out. I feel if you contact this Harry guy, through him this whole mess can be salvaged—without lawsuits. But you have to act on it immediately."

"But what about Evans?"

"Sorry, Bill, but I'm going to make you use your own intuition to answer that. So close your eyes, take a deep breath."

"Ah, come on, Dawnea."

I ignored him, saying, "Take a deep breath, let it out."

He gave in and started breathing.

"Good. Now continue, another . . . then another . . . one more . . . See the giant screen in front of you. See Evans on the screen."

Bill's body jolted when I asked him to see Mr. Evans. He sighed. "Okay, okay, I see the bastard."

"Bill . . ."

"Okay, sorry, I see him."

"Good. Now see Evans, Harry, and you sitting at a restaurant talking things out. I want you to listen to the three of you batting the project around. I want you to see the resolution. I want you to see this film finished and out there. I want you to see your name on this film and, last but not least, I want you to see the money in the bank."

Several minutes passed, then Bill opened his eyes.

I asked, "Got it?"

He smiled. "Yeah, I saw Harry calling Evans, setting up the meeting. We were at the Ivy, having lunch. I could hear the three of us screaming it out. Then I heard Evans say something that just made me feel like an egotistical ass. He said he'd never wanted credit over me, he just wanted to make a good film. Shit, it just blew me away."

I laughed softly and replied, "Yeah, well, the ego can be a powerful thing. Almost always, if it feels threatened, it will go for the kill."

He blushed through to the roots of his hair.

"Hey, Bill, to err is human, to forgive divine. Now go, make the phone call, and put the thing into motion."

Bill left a message for me later that afternoon. The

meeting was set. I knew the outcome would be exactly as he and I had seen.

It was. The film made millions. Bill and Mr. Evans went on to make three more pictures together. As I said, "To forgive is divine!"

I met Barbara at the door to my office. Was this the same woman I had worked with two months ago? Unlike the haggard woman who had been here last, she was tan, radiant, and it seemed her feet were barely touching the ground as she walked in and sat down.

"Okay, Barb, dish: Tell me what has happened to you. You look completely transformed."

She laughed a sly little laugh. "Well, remember the last time I was here?"

How well I did. Her eye had been black and blue, her mouth swollen, and there had been bruises on her arms. Ugh, recalling how badly she had been abused by her husband made my blood boil.

"Yes, I remember that day very well."

"I left your office with determination. I was going to get a restraining order and then I was going to go after the bastard. I was terrified, but I was going to do it. I would no longer run from him or allow him to terrify me.

"Well, I did all of those things. I hired someone to look into our affairs, and, boy, did I find out some things. All these years, he'd been hiding money from me, money I'd earned as well. As you know, I let him take control of everything. Anyway, when he found out I knew about everything, he threatened to kill me. I was still terrified of him, but I didn't back down. I let my attorneys handle the communication with him. For the first time in my life I began to feel as though there was hope."

I nodded approvingly, once again reminded of some people's courage. "Good for you, Barbara."

She smiled and said, "I haven't even gotten to the good part yet. Anyway, I wanted to go somewhere for a while. I couldn't make up my mind whether to visit my sister in Texas or say the hell with it and go to Greece."

"Why Greece?"

"I remembered what you said about the intuitive mind. It told me to go to Greece. I checked to see if I had any nervousness about it, and I didn't."

I listened to Barbara, watching her animated face.

"So, off I go to Greece." She added, "On my husband's credit card."

I chuckled to myself. "I'd say you'd earned a trip on him."

She pounded her fist on the chair and shouted, "Damned right I did. Anyway, while I was in Greece, I met the most wonderful man. He was there on vacation. The man you described to me in the last session."

I raised my eyebrows and gasped. "Wow! That was quick."

She sighed, saying, "For all the years of abuse I'd endured with Chas, I'd say it couldn't happen fast enough. Anyway, he lives in New York. He is a commodities trader and, Dawnea—not that I care—but he is loaded with money. And sexy, he is so sexy. Mind you, he's in his fifties, but he doesn't look a day over forty. I feel so safe with him. I never believed I could have happiness, I thought I would never at my age. . . ."

My vanity kicked in and I chided her, "Hey, now, Barbara, you are five years younger than me."

"Well, anyway, if I had not followed my intuition, if I had been the old Barbara who was motivated by fear, I would have never gone to Greece, never met this man. So, you see, it works. Just like you said: 'When you listen with pure intent, it works.' "

"Dawnea, I was so excited, I had to call you and tell you what happened."

"So tell me, Robert, tell me."

"Well, you know the last time I was in for a session and we did that phasing thing about intuition?"

"Yes."

"Well, you know I was torn between moving back to Jersey or staying here and taking one last stab at trying to get financing for my project."

"Come on, Robert, I can't stand it—what's happening?" His excitement was contagious. It was driving me nuts.

"Okay, I phased, doing it just the way we did here: the lake, the peaceful thing, the whole deal. Then I put the question out. Am I going to get funding for this project, and if so, where or who? Well, let me tell you, no sooner did I speak those words when I got the face of this woman I'd met last week while I was picking up my dry cleaning. We'd had this little conversation, and she had invited me out for coffee, but I hadn't called her back.

"As soon as I saw her face in my phasing, I rummaged through the trash for her number."

Even though we were on the phone, I could "see" his grinning face. I could hear that grin in his voice. "All right, I'll cut to the chase."

"Good idea, Robert."

"I had coffee with her. Actually, we spent the better part of the day together. And she loved the project. She just happens to be one of the head developers for HBO. She took the project in the door. They're going to do it and I got an advance. A hefty one. Think of it! I was one fraction of a second away from quitting, and here I am, deal and money in hand. Man, I am in hog heaven."

"Robert, is that Harley heaven or pig's?"

He let out a bellowing laugh. "Oh, and yeah," he continued, "the money for our last three sessions is in the mail. Thanks, Dawnea. Man, this life is great, isn't it?"

"Yep, from now on I'll bet you'll be phasing on a regular basis."

"You know it."

Using this phase will become as natural to you as breathing. Just like Robert, Barbara, and Bill you will have a few hits and misses until you totally begin to trust that "Voice." But once you do, you will use it every day of your life with great success. I use it every single day—and if it works for me, it will definitely work for you. You are no different from me; you just haven't had as much practice.

Remember Kevin's dad in *Field of Dreams?* Let the now, right here—today—be your heaven. Allow yourself to listen to the phenomenal you inside yourself.

Create your heaven right here on earth. Live your Chosen Destiny. Allow yourself to be ignited by the Divine Spark. Listen to your intuition, and most of all, *make your dreams come true*!!!

Are You Ready for a Miracle?

He that believeth in me,
these works that I do
shall he do also.

The Master Jesus

Back when I was growing up, it was very big with all of the evangelists to have people queue up in a "prayer line" for "hands-on" healing. And despite the fact that the preachers themselves weren't coming from a place of truth, I watched in fascination as folks standing in that prayer line were touched, and to my never-ending surprise many of those folks were actually healed. Not only did they receive an emotional healing, but a physical one as well.

We're talkin' about the blind-seeing, lame-walking, cancer-vanishing kind of healing. I witnessed many "miracles" back then in those revival meetings.

How, you ask, is this possible? I hear you say, "Come on, Dawnea, if the preacher laying his hands on that person in the prayer line was a fake, how could he heal?"

He couldn't. It was the people's faith that healed

them. The absolute knowing that before that evangelist ever put his hands on them, before he or she ever "prayed over" them, they would be healed.

I've seen it, time and time again, not only in those prayer lines, but every day in my life—and so have you. Think about people around your life who have been "cured" of a disease.

For that matter, think about the word *disease* for a moment. Let's break it down: *dis* and *ease.* That's right; your body, your mind, your emotions, are out of whack. To heal yourself is to bring your body, mind, and emotions back into balance. To *know* that you can. To *not* come from a place of fear about the results your doctor has just told to you, but coming from a place of *knowing* that you are capable of moving beyond the doctor's diagnosis. That you can move beyond that death sentence, move way beyond the fear that wants to literally eat you alive.

I have been doing "hands-on" work for most of my life. I've worked on many different kinds of diseases. I've witnessed "miracles" in my practice countless times. I am filled with so much respect for those brave people when I recall the amount of courage it took to seek out an alternative way to their healing.

They have regained their health by being and living conscious of what is good for their bodies and what is not. None of us should ever take our bodies for granted. Abuse of one's body is abuse to one's soul. Especially for those of you who have a dormant disease hanging out in there. Get real! If you say, "Fuck it," go out, and drink a fifth of Jack Daniel's or twenty martinis at happy hour; if you do drugs or smoke ten packs of cigarettes a day; or live on Twinkies or Ding Dongs; your body will reward you accordingly.

If you "buy into" fear—the kind of fear that says, "Your body is going to waste away," or "You deserve to be sick—after all, look at the life you've chosen to live"—you're buying into a power that allows disease to run rampant. That fear—yours and others'—will begin to "eat you alive."

Please understand how powerful your mind is. As we've seen, the mind can make real what your emotions create—in your life and in your body. Where your emotions lead, your thoughts follow. And those thoughts are living things, which gain added power when you obsess about them. I don't know exactly why this is, but that gut-wrenching kind of fear is potent. So potent, it will begin to rule your life.

The power is yours to reclaim. Determine that you will not allow anything in your consciousness except Divine Mind's love for you, you as a precious child of the Universe. Allow that love to fill you each and every moment of every day. That love is the most powerful healing tool that exists. You are a reflection of the Divine Creator, and in that you are perfect in all ways. Right here, right now, know that you are perfection, and by living as a reflection of that Infinite Source, you need never be ravaged.

I have worked extensively with many diseases, including cancer and, most terrifyingly, AIDS. Those clients who have stayed healthy, stayed beautiful, are the ones who have taken control over their lives, who have refused to be ruled by fear. They have heeded my counsel regarding conscious living. They know that they are a child of Divine Mind just like everyone else down here on this planet!!!

Your consciousness dictates everything your body does. Right down to the cellular level. If you harbor a belief that you are going to contract a disease, your body will oblige you by creating that disease inside of it.

If you believe that you deserve to live down here on this earth with a healthy body, if you love yourself as much as the Divine loves you and you reflect that love by revering the temple (your body) that your soul is lodged in, it will reward you by giving you long-lasting life, perfect health, and inner joy.

I know what you're thinking. *What about reality here, Dawnea? I live a damn stressful life.* Then you bloody well better find a way to vent that stress. (Phasing is great for this.)

Most people completely ignore their body until it screams back at them for attention (i.e., disease). So get busy, honor your body, and it will honor you.

Steve Martin's movie *Leap of Faith* is one of the best depictions of those old-time gospel tent meetings I have ever seen. (Bear in mind that I grew up with that stuff; cut my teeth on an altar bench, you might say.)

The movie begins with Steve's big semi breaking down in this poor little farm town that has been ravaged by lack of rain. He decides to "set up" his revival meeting right there—much to the chagrin of the local sheriff (Liam Neeson).

Steve is determined to get this little waitress to pay attention to him. It just so happens her younger brother was tragically disabled in an accident; hit by a drunk driver, he has lost most of the use of his legs. There is one scene where the boy is lifting weights, telling Jonas (Steve Martin) that it is God's will if he is to be healed, when Jonas spits back, "You have something to say about it too. Better get out there and do everything you can, boy."

Toward the end of the movie Jonas is onstage, doing his "laying on of hands." Previously there had been a small miracle that Jonas "artistically" created: The large crucifix used in the big tent had miraculously changed overnight; the eyes of Jesus, formerly closed, were now open—because Jonas had repainted them while the town and the night guard slept.

The people are in awe of this man who brought miracles to their little town. You can feel the tension in the air as you watch Boyd (the injured boy), with the aid of crutches, walk onstage for his healing. Struggling, Boyd walks over to the cross, touches Jesus' feet, and by a true miracle, drops his crutches and begins walking unassisted.

Did Jonas heal Boyd? No, absolutely not. Boyd's faith in a greater power and the collective consciousness of all those people in that tent, believing, are what healed that young man.

Now, are you ready to begin your healing? Let's phase!!!

Set the scene with some music. This is a phase where you can use some blues or gospel music—or whatever it takes to get you to feel like gettin' into your soul. (The part of you that *knows* you are perfect in *all* ways.)

Sit comfortably and do your circular breathing. See the giant movie screen in your mind. The music is playing in the background, you have done your circular breathing, and are on your way to phasing.

See yourself up there on that screen. You are lying in a field of swaying green grass. It is springtime. Listen . . . listen to the earth as it speaks to you. The earth is waking up from a long, dark winter. Indications of life are everywhere, surrounding you. The ground beneath you is reaching up to fill your body with strength; the grass around you is whispering in the gentle breeze, "Alive, alive, you are here, you are alive, and isn't it joyous?" Your heart begins to beat in time with the aliveness of your surroundings. Tiny birds are chirping their songs; all is speaking of newness, of aliveness, of beauty. Your beauty and the earth's beauty. Above you the sun is shining, caressing your face with light, with warmth, with healing.

Now, as you watch this scene you have created on that giant screen up there, I want you to feel what you are seeing. As you see your body lying in this grassy field, I want you to see someone approaching you. The closer they get, the more you *feel* their presence. This someone is your healer. Your healer can be a man or a woman. You seem to recognize this person in some manner, yet you cannot place him. He—or she—is whatever you see, however vague in your memory. Trust him. He has come to assist you in healing your body of any unwanted debris.

As the healer approaches you on the screen, he bends down and gently, so gently, takes your weary head and lays it in his healing hands. Immediately, you feel an electrical current begin to flow into you. You feel that healing current as you are watching yourself on that screen. It enters into your body as you are sitting there observing, and you are deeply touched. At this moment you are living in "suspended disbelief." That is: the "you" watching becomes the "you" on the screen.

The healer gently touches your heart. The gentleness of his touch reaches right into your body, into your emotions. You take a deep, ragged breath, soaking in all of the love the healer is transferring to you.

He continues to work on your body, filling it with the Divine's healing love, releasing all old pent-up pain, old pent-up frustration. Any and all "dis-ease" that exists in your body is freed now as you bask in the healer's touch.

The healer sits with you, gently holding your hand. You feel that electrical healing of energy flowing from him, through him to you. Your body, your mind, your emotions, are connected to your soul. You are at peace, you are at one with yourself and the world. You feel as though you have awakened from a long, restful sleep. You are completely rejuvenated.

The healer turns his face to look at the you who is sitting in the chair watching the screen. Who is he? Could that face be your own? Do you, indeed, have it within your grasp to heal yourself? Trust whatever comes to you right now.

Allow the screen in your mind to disappear. Open your eyes, stretch out; you feel as though you have just had a long, restful sleep. You are completely rejuvenated. The feeling remains with you!!

I slumped on my knees as I pulled the door to my treatment room shut. Couldn't have the client on the treatment table seeing me buckling under the current of energy that had just passed through me to heal her. I sat against the wall, gulping in deep breaths of air. I knew I shouldn't have worked today; I had the beginning of a nasty flu. Everyone around me had it. I had bought into "catching it." And, of course, since I had spoken those fateful words just the day before, "I'll probably be the next to come down with it," my body was living it out.

However, diehard that I am, I knew that this woman desperately needed this session. It had taken her six long months to get the courage to come and see me. The phasing session we had just finished was one of the more powerful ones I had done to date. Grace, too, had an evangelical background, having grown up in the South. She'd been convinced by her fanatical aunt that she was and would always be "full of the devil." She even brought me drawings of what "lived" inside her. It never ceases to amaze me how people's minds work. How they manifest in their lives things they've been *programmed* to believe exist. Grace did not have "the devil" inside her. She did, however, have seven disincarnate entities (spirits that hover around the earth plane for whatever reason and refuse to make the transition to the other side) living in her body. Psychiatrists would call this a multiple-personality disorder, but that is not what this was. There were entities living inside of this woman. Five men, two women, and one lonely little girl. They were real and they were tormenting Grace (and had been for many years).

One by one they appeared on the giant screen in Grace's mind. One by one she was able to let them go. She demanded they leave her body, leave her life, and go their own way. We both watched as, one by one, they did as Grace willed them. The look of peace that came over this woman's face when she'd finished phasing was so amazing, so incredibly beautiful. She looked like she was thirteen years old again. I knew she would be able to live her life outside my treatment room in peace.

But there I sat on the floor, my body breaking out in a cold sweat, my throat on fire, my muscles feeling as though I had spent fifty hours in the gym. I wanted to lie down right there on the floor and go to sleep. Instead, I took a deep breath and brought up the giant screen in my mind. I saw the healer laying cool hands on my burning forehead. I felt a soothing, healing light wash over me; I bathed in that healing glow. I thought I had remained seated there for hours, but when I went to wash my hands, I glanced at the clock and noticed barely five minutes had passed.

My clamminess was gone, my muscles no longer felt

like someone had had me on the rack. I had no fever. I was fine. Yeah!!! Let's hear it for phasing!!!

Trent sat wide eyed, staring at me, waiting to see exactly what I was going to do, what I would say.

I closed my eyes, took a deep breath. Having already "phased" on him earlier, I knew why he was there.

"So, Trent, how long ago were you diagnosed HIV positive?" I asked.

His face had turned pasty white, his eyes now looking so large and so blue next to the pallor of his skin (which, by the way, two minutes ago, had been deeply tanned).

He croaked, "Three, uh . . . a little over three months ago."

I shook my head and told him, "Yes, I see it. It's microscopic." I sighed. Every time I saw this disease, I wanted to scream.

I saw this disease for the first time many years ago, before people really knew what AIDS was. I was working with a young man who had been diagnosed with cancer. Or so he told me. I'd been working for quite some time with clients who had cancer, and I knew that to me, as a telepath, cancer looks like Pac-Men with teeth. What this young man had looked completely different, a steel-toothed microbe, racing like a Tasmanian devil through his body, ravaging everything that it could. The more it ravaged, the more it wanted.

Of all the diseases I have encountered and worked

with, by far the AIDS virus is the most challenging. I've seen it in its early stages and I have seen it far advanced. The thing it feeds on—like all diseases, only more so—is fear. Not only does it feed on the fear of the person who has contracted the AIDS virus, it feeds on society's fear of it as well.

When AIDS is dormant, telepathically it looks microscopic. When it's in its advanced stage, it does look like a Tasmanian devil with those knives for teeth, cutting away at the immune system, at the body.

Those of you reading this who have been diagnosed HIV positive, know this: Despite what you may have heard, or seen, you do not have to die; you do not have to lose your precious body or your health. You can live a full life without ever awakening that sharp-toothed devil.

Now here I was, so many years later, looking at this gorgeous young man, looking into his terrified eyes.

"Trent, let me make something real clear to you. Just because you have contracted AIDS does not mean you are going to die. I want you to phase with me right now."

"What's that, Dawnea?"

"I'll show you, it's real easy. Together, we are going to look into your future. It's not enough for me to tell you you're going to be fine—healthy—five, ten, or more years down the road, I want you to see it for yourself. Ready?"

Trent nodded his head, his eyes remaining glued to mine.

I smiled, saying, "You're going to have to close your eyes." I watched him close his eyes, watched his hands relax.

"Okay, I want you to just take a deep breath, in through your nose, out through your mouth." I took Trent through the circular breathing.

"Trent, see a giant movie screen inside your mind, in front of you. Do you see it?"

He was quiet for a few moments, so I asked, "Trent, do you see the screen?"

"Yeah, I see it. I feel like I'm sitting at the Cinerama Dome."

I hadn't heard that one before. How cool, we were onto something here. "Trent, I want you to see yourself on that screen eight years from now. What are you doing?"

He started laughing, a rich, throaty laugh. "I'm climbing. I've always wanted to go to Tibet and climb the Himalayas, and that is exactly what I am doing."

Before I could ask more, he went right on.

"I'm in great shape. Hey, my new lover is with me. I guess this one is going to last. God, I love this. Can I see more, Dawnea?"

I smiled, thinking how I wish everyone would jump into phasing like this young man. (That goes for you too.)

"Yeah, look ahead . . . fifteen years—where are you?"

"Successful in my advertising business, traveling a lot, enjoying life a hell of a lot more than I do now."

"Trent, are you taking care of yourself?"

"Yes, yes, I am."

"Trent, how do you feel about what you are seeing on that screen?"

"Relieved," he answered.

"Good, let the screen disappear, open your eyes."

I've seen Trent, on and off, for the last nine years. He has climbed the Himalayas and he is in the best of health.

Sasha was lying on my treatment table, ready for our phasing session.

She grabbed my hand and began to anxiously ask, "Dawnea . . ."

"I know, Sasha, I know how important this is to you."

"Dawnea, the doctor told me I had to have a hysterectomy. He said that the damage done to my cervix and my uterus from the years of sexual abuse couldn't be healed. He said there are fibrous cysts in my uterus and that my entire female area looks like a breeding ground for cancer." Sasha's voice caught in her throat as she continued. "He wants it taken care of immediately."

Ugh. I bit back the words of anger on the tip of my tongue. How many times had I seen this, heard this, before? "No other alternative but to 'cut out her female organs. . . .' " I took a long, steady breath as I gently touched Sasha's face, asking, "How do you feel about that, Sasha?"

Her voice quivered as she told me, "You know how I feel about my past. The men, the money, the 'profession.'"

I shook my head, blew out a breath of frustration, thinking how hard people are on themselves. "Sasha, the Master Jesus forgave Mary Magdalene. You can forgive yourself. And you don't have to cut out your female organs to do it."

Sasha squeezed my hand tightly.

I sat down at the head of the treatment table and I cradled her head in my hands. "Sasha, I want you to see the giant screen in your mind."

Dreamily, she whispered, "Yes, I see it."

"Now I want you to see yourself standing naked on that screen. Look at how beautiful you are. Look at how precious your body is."

Sasha winced.

With authority in my voice I scolded her, "Sasha, don't even think of going there. Your body is yours. No one can possess it. I want you to take it back. Do it now, damn it!!"

A tear trickled down her cheek into my hands.

"Sasha?"

A knowingness filled her voice as she answered, "Yes, I see myself as I am. A perfect, unspoiled child of God."

Joy filled my heart as I responded, "Good, now see your uterus, your cervix. See your ovaries." I moved from the top of the table, gently removing my hands from underneath her head, placing them on Sasha's lower abdomen.

"See the area I am touching completely filled with golden light. The golden light of healing."

She began to take deep breaths as though she were breathing in the light.

"Good work." I could see and feel the festering in her ovaries and uterus heal. I could see her cervix absorbing the golden light. It was going well.

Out loud, I continued. "Now see yourself on that giant screen going to that same doctor to be tested. See him giving you the results. All cysts, any foreign substances, are gone. Completely gone."

Excitement filled her voice as she described the scene. "I see his face. He's in shock."

"Good, you've done good work here, be proud of yourself. Allow the screen to disappear. Just relax, let me finish working on you."

Several months passed before I received a call from Sasha. "Dawnea, I just wanted you to know that I continued to work with the phasing tape we did together, and guess what? I got married, and you know what? You won't believe it." She rushed on. "I am pregnant. So much for the doctor's diagnosis. Yep, I am pregnant. The doctor told me I could never have a child because of the shape my uterus, ovaries, and cervix were in."

Not allowing me to comment, she barreled on. "Oh, sorry I never called you until now. I went back to him after our phasing session. Everything was gone. He didn't believe it. He X-rayed me five times to be sure. It was completely hilarious. I can't wait to tell Dr. Steidman I am with child."

I was beaming from ear to ear. "Sasha, honey, that is great. Congratulations."

Ah, when people take their power back, anything can happen. Absolutely anything.

"Dawnea, Rachel asked me to call you about my back. I have to leave for France in five hours. I can hardly walk."

"Rachel asked you to call me? What about you, James? I never work with someone unless they are ready."

"I'm not sure I believe in what you do, but I am in so much pain right now, I'm willing to try anything. Besides, I can't get in touch with my chiropractor."

I had to count to ten before responding. "James, it's Sunday, I've worked my ass off all week. If you are coming in, you damn well better be ready to go to work on your back. You don't have to believe in what I do, but you do have to want your back to be free of pain."

"Oh . . . I want it, I want it. This has been going on for over ten years."

James showed up at my home bent over like a ninety-year-old man. Had he not been in so much pain, I would have laughed at the sight of him: this big macho guy all hunched over.

I took his arm and led him straight to my treatment room. "James, can you get on the table?"

He nodded his head yes, moaning as he slid his body up on the table.

"Take a deep breath. Just let me work on you for a while."

I headed right for the red aura I saw coming out of his back through his sweatshirt, oozing like blood. I put my hands on him and closed my eyes, willing the giant screen to appear. When it did, I told him, "James, I want you to work with me. While your eyes are closed, see a giant movie screen in your mind."

He stuttered, "What? What in the hell are you talking about?"

I was losing patience. "Do as I say, James. Do it or I will send you out of here just like you came in."

"Okay, okay already, I'm doing it. I see the screen. So?"

"So, see yourself on the screen with your back to us. Your skin is transparent, we are looking at your lower back. What do you see?"

"Huh . . . I see the third disk from the bottom, it has like a pinched nerve or something that looks like a red string—it's trapped between the second and third disk."

Since I saw exactly the same thing, I said, "Hey, you might live. That's right. That red string is why you are in agony. Now watch carefully. As I put my hands on your back, right where those disks are, I want you to see that string release from those two disks."

I placed my hands right where the glowing red was on his back. "James, work with me on this, see the red string gone, feel yourself letting go of the pain in your back."

It took James (the "doubting Thomas") over an hour to let go of that pain. But let go of it he did. When he finally let go, he shouted, "Hey, I'm dancing . . . well, that is . . . the guy on the screen is dancing." He opened his eyes and marveled, "It's gone!!! Dawnea, the pain is completely gone. I don't know how this stuff works, but the pain is gone."

It's been five years down the road and I've never spoken to James again. I either see Rachel in my office or speak with her on the telephone about every six months. She tells me that even though he denies ever having come to see me and refuses to talk about anything that happened that day, James hasn't been back to his chiropractor since.

All of these people are examples of how phasing for healing the body can work. The most important thing to remember about this particular phase is that you have to want your own healing. You have to be willing to let go of the drama created by your pain and your fear of disease.

I hear you saying, "But, Dawnea, I *am* ready." But are you really? We get a lot of emotional mileage out of suffering. I know that sounds weird, but think about it. . . . Now, this moment, let that suffering go. Allow Divine Mind to connect with your emotions, allow yourself to bask in that love. Put your trust in your own ability to hear, as well as knowing that Divine Mind sees you as perfect. Perfect in every way.

When you truly connect to Divine Mind, you will connect to that immense love for you. You will know you are loved; you are part of a much bigger picture than suffering, than "dis ease." When you are ready to do that, you can work on healing your body. It is the only body you have. Honor it, cherish, and—above all—take the best care of it. If you do that, it will reward you by moving through life pain free, disease free, no matter what your age.

You are a walking miracle right now. Just think about what an amazing thing the human body is. Even more amazing is you and the power of faith, imagination, the power of healing!!!

Remember those revival meetings. Why were some people healed while others went away with their pain, their illnesses? After years of working with people myself, I can only say this: There is a moment in someone's life when they surrender up the painful drama they've been living. When they choose faith instead of doubt and skepticism; joy instead of pain; love instead of fear; and life instead of dying inside every day. And when that moment happens inside you, that moment will be the beginning of your life. The healing you deserve, the healing you have ached for—how long have you waited? That healing can begin.

Everyone has his or her own safety net. If you choose to use the standard Western medical approach for treatment when you are ill, and you are under a doctor's care—honor that. You can still phase for your healing and work with your doctor. Phasing will speed up the healing process. Why? Because you are cooperating with your doctor *and* the part of you that wants to be healed. Through phasing you can assist the doctor by helping yourself.

The Never-Ending Story

Traveling through my mind
I took so many roads
All of them led me here
None of them were wrong
I wanna bless myself
For listening to my heart
I'm gonna live in happiness
I'm gonna start to live in
Joy, joy, joy in my soul

From the song "Joy"
Words by Molly Pasutti

The soul never dies. The body gives way, but the soul—our soul—lives on through all eternity. When we choose to leave earth, we return to where we began. We return to love—the Divine's unconditional love for us.

Phase Ten is about two things: It's about connecting ourselves to that Divine Love—right here, right now—and living in that state of grace that comes with loving ourselves as unconditionally as the Divine loves us.

Phase Ten is also going to give you the phasing tools to reach loved ones who have gone over to Spirit Side. You will be able to connect with them and you will feel their connection to the Divine's love and to you.

*   *   *

Put on your music. Sit comfortably. Exhale your breath through your mouth. Take a deep breath in through your nose, hold it to the count of seven, release it through your mouth. Repeat this breathing seven times. On the seventh out breath, begin phasing.

See the giant screen in front of you. See yourself on that screen. Larger than life, you are up there on that screen. Look at yourself. What is your body stance? What is the expression on your face? How does the you that is sitting there watching feel about the you that is up there on the screen? Take a moment to ponder this.

As you are watching yourself on the giant screen, a beautiful rainbow-colored light beams down on you. At first it is like a spotlight, beaming directly down on you. As the light permeates the you on the screen, the other you sitting there is filled with longing. Feel the light filling you. See the light expand to reach you too. Feel yourself merge with the you on the screen. Now the entire screen is filled with radiance.

You are filled with this radiance. Waves and waves of love wash over you. Your whole being is washed with this love. Such tenderness, such compassion, as you have never felt, is filling your mind, your soul, your body, and your spirit. Allow yourself to completely surrender to the beautiful light of love.

Now that you have connected yourself to Divine's love, let's go back to the giant screen in your mind. On the screen is an aerial view of a beautiful valley. As the camera zooms closer, you see the valley's lushness. Human hands have never touched this place. The trees are many—every size, shape, texture. The lush foliage grows everywhere. See yourself on the screen, walking through the richness of this valley. Merge your emotions with the you on the screen, experiencing the beauty, the sacredness, of this place. You can smell the rich earth; you gently touch the foliage as you walk by.

From a distance you hear a waterfall. Walk toward it. You cannot see it, you can only hear the thundering water. The closer you get, the louder the sound of the water becomes until, brushing back the branch of an ancient tree, you are there.

The sun is beaming down on the waterfall, casting rainbow prisms of light. Without a thought you dive in. Standing underneath the pounding water, you allow it to wash over you, to heal you. To set your heart and your mind free.

You rise out of the water, lie down on the warm grass, close your eyes. You are at peace, at peace with all that is.

After a time you hear a voice calling your name. You are in total trust, and you follow that voice. It leads you to a clearing.

The person you are looking for is in that clearing. The one who has gone over to Spirit Side is standing there, lovingly awaiting your arrival.

You walk up to the Spirit, embrace, and you feel the Spirit's love reaching out to you. (You see, when you go to Spirit Side, ego is gone; all that remains is Divine Truth, Divine Love.)

In even stride you walk together. During the walk you speak of the past. Of a time past, a time when you were both still on earth. Tell that person everything you were not able to say.

And listen while that person tells you everything you never got the chance to hear before.

Open your heart, let the healing be complete.

In the movie *Ghost,* Sam (Patrick Swayze) is murdered. Senselessly, violently murdered.

His spirit is trapped on earth. He feels he cannot leave until he knows his wife, Molly (Demi Moore), is safe and until the truth is told. Through the help of a woman (Whoopi Goldberg) who is, much to her surprise, able to communicate with his spirit, Sam saves his wife.

The last scene of the movie is so beautiful. The light has come to take Sam to the other side. You see the light as it beams down: beautiful rays and tiny sparkling prisms of light. You can feel the love as you look at the light on that giant screen. Just before he goes, Sam looks at Molly and says, "It's amazing, the love inside, you take it with you."

I sat waiting for my client to arrive. It had been a long day of sessions. I took a deep breath, willing myself to go to my center, and then I heard it. A sound like teardrops falling on a pool of water. I heard my mother's voice calling me. I watched as an outline of her spirit appeared before me. She held out her hand and said, "Honey, I am so sorry I was never there for you. I promise you this: That which I never did for you in my life, I will do for you in my death."

My mother had the gift of sight. But for her it was this dark, dark thing that would reach out and grab her. I remember that once, in the brief time I lived with her, she woke up screaming, "No, no, no." The next day we got a call that my uncle had died. Being a triple Scorpio, I don't think she knew how to harness the energy that came at her and through her.

When I was eighteen I received a phone call that my mother was in critical condition in the hospital. I rushed to where she was. When I arrived, my brother George ran to me, throwing his arms around me, sobbing. "She finally did it," he said, his voice broken with pain.

"How bad is it, Georgie?"

He winced. "She blew the whole front of her skull off. She was lucky. The gun was pointed sideways, so instead of her face it was her forehead and all the bone up there."

I hugged him tight as he wept and told me, "D, I found her right after she did it. I walked in the house as she fell onto the bathroom floor."

Tears sprang to my eyes as I comforted him. "I'm so sorry, Georgie, I am so sorry."

A nurse came out of the room and asked, "Is Connie Decker's daughter here?"

I answered, "Yes, I am her daughter."

"Your mother wants to see you."

I followed the nurse to the room where my mother lay in darkness. As soon as I stepped inside, my mother

whispered, "Come close." She looked so small and fragile lying there; her head was all bandaged, her small
arms were outside of the covers. She looked like a little
refugee lying in that big bed. I fought back the tears.

She reached out her hand to me. I took it. Her fingers
were like a little girl's. She kept her eyes closed as,
barely above a whisper, she said, "Listen, in case I don't
live through this, I want you to know that even though I
left you with your grandmother when you were just a
baby, even though I never fought your father for you, I
love you. I love you so much that I knew it would be
better for you if you didn't live with me.

"I'm just not right in the head, honey. You were better off with him." (She knew nothing of those years of
pain I spent with that man and his wife.)

The tears rolled down my face. I looked at her lying
there, so tiny, so fragile. But, despite it all, her spirit was
so strong, I knew she would survive this.

Survive she did. The doctors put a steel plate in her
head.

She lived for several years after the incident. It was
when my stepfather, her life mate, died that she made
transition. Two months after his death, she went in for
surgery to have the steel plate in her head replaced. She
died on the operating table.

When her spirit came to me that night, I wasn't surprised. I knew she would not stay on earth without Al-
vin, my stepfather.

After the night she appeared to me, my own telepathic gifts increased. I have learned to harness them.

She gave me a great gift in her passing. I often feel her near me. Bless you, Momma. I love you too.

Mary, Susie, and their mother, June, sat in my office. The three of them were at odds with each other. They had come for a session today to sort things out.

"But, Mom, you knew about it. You knew about Dad and you never stopped him. You never stopped him from touching us, from doing those horrible things to us. How could you let him do that, Mom?" Mary's angry voice spat out those words.

June, heavily weeping, sat in the chair across from the girls.

A week before, June had been to see me. Her husband had passed over to Spirit Side two months earlier. She was desperately trying to sort out her feelings.

"Yes, I'll admit it. I knew. But I was so afraid to say anything. I couldn't take care of you girls by myself, I had no career, no way of earning money, and you know your father, he was always threatening to turn us out on our ear. I was terrified."

My heart went out to the three of them sitting there. Such unresolved conflict.

"Well, I hope he rots in hell!" Susie's delicate voice was filled with rage as she said it.

Those words were barely out of her mouth when I felt her father's presence in the room. His grief was as thick as the fog bank surrounding my home.

I looked over at the girls and asked, "Did you have an

opportunity to face your father with any of this before he died?"

Both, in unison, said, "No, we didn't. He was ill one day, then the next thing we knew, he was in intensive care."

"Did you visit him there?"

"Yes, we visited. Only once, and for a brief moment he came to and acknowledged us."

"Susie, what happened?"

She hesitated, looking at Mary for approval, then said, "He opened his eyes, one small tear came out. But who knows for sure? Maybe he didn't know it was us, and maybe his eyes were just watering."

"June, what do you think?"

"Dawnea, in all his life he never admitted what he did to the girls. The day before he died, I was determined to at least get him to say it to me. I sat next to his bed, held his hand, spoke softly in his ear. When I began speaking of the past, of the girls, he jerked his hand away." She sighed the sigh of the heavy emotional burden she was bearing.

"Girls, how long have you been seeing me?"

June spoke. "Six years."

"And in that six years, have I been accurate?"

"Yes, in everything, Dawnea."

"Okay, what if I were to tell you your father is here in this room, that he is standing next to me, and he wants you to tell him how you feel about him."

June piped up, "What does he look like?"

I chuckled to myself as I told her, "He's about six feet

tall, receding hairline—no, a bald spot he combs his hair over. He has a ruddy complexion, is big around the belly. He has dark brown eyes."

The girls raised their eyebrows. "That's him, all right."

"Okay, now's your chance. I want you both to close your eyes. Take a deep breath, let it go. I want you to see a giant screen in front of you. On that screen see your father. Do you see him?"

"Yes," they both replied.

"Okay, let it rip. Tell him everything you did not get the chance to say while he was alive. Get it all out."

They did. First one girl, then the other, spoke her truth to their father. They went from anger and rage, to tears and silence.

"June, now it's your turn. Breathe, see that giant screen in your mind. See your husband on that screen. What do you have to say to him?"

"Nothing, I have nothing to say to him, I said it all before he died. . . . Oh, there is one thing: 'Dave, I am free of you and I will sell the house. I will have a life and I will love again.'"

The girls chimed in, "Right on, Mom."

I saw Dave's spirit breathe a sigh of relief. He left the room as soon as he'd heard June's words.

Susie softly asked, "He left, didn't he, Dawnea?"

"Yes, for now. But if there is anything else you need to say to him, sit yourself down, see him on the screen in your mind, and say it."

*   *   *

I heard from June several months later. Indeed, she had sold the house and joined a group of people who enjoyed traveling. She was making new friends. For the first time in twenty-three years she was living her life. She had not met "the man" yet, but I knew it was only a matter of time.

Mary and Susie started their own catering company and it's doing very well. Mary lost twenty pounds and Susie began seeing a lovely man. So much healing had taken place that day in my office.

Closure on the past is a powerful thing!!!

Jeannine's serene face greeted me as I walked into my office and sat down; this was not the norm for this woman. I'd been counseling Jeannine for five years, and our sessions always began with deep emotional work.

"You look so peaceful, Jeannine, tell me. . . ."

"Dawnea, I had the most beautiful experience. You know my aunt has been ill. The last time I was here, we talked about her leaving, going to the other side. In our last session together you asked me to see her passing filled with love, remember?"

I nodded, recalling the session we'd had. It had been almost entirely about this dear woman, who was well into her nineties.

Jeannine went on. "A few days ago my mother and I went to visit her. I remember as a little girl, loving her so much. She was so different from the rest of the family. She was so loving, so nonjudgmental; and she was fun. She would get down on the floor and play jacks with us. One summer she let us use all of her good sheets to build houses in her backyard. And she let us sleep outside in those wobbly houses we built. In the morning she brought doughnuts and hot chocolate. She was so accepting of who we were as children. Unlike my own mother, who criticized everything I did, my aunt Helen accepted me for who I was.

"She and my mother did not get along. Mother always looked down her nose at Aunt Helen's 'funny ways.' Truth is, I think she was jealous of my aunt. But because my mother didn't like Aunt Helen, I was allowed to spend very little time with her. You know how it is, years pass and families drift apart."

I nodded my head in agreement, thinking how long I'd been estranged from my own family.

Jeannine's eyes filled with tears as she said, "Dawnea, it was so beautiful. My aunt was like a little child. She was so open to all of us, so gentle. I watched as she and my cousins played games together. They laughed, they held hands, they were so loving to one another.

"One day, we were all in the middle of a game with Aunt Helen, when she stopped and looked at something none of us could see. Her face was filled with such love, such radiance."

As I listened, I could see her aunt's face. I knew what she was looking at. "Jeannine, did you ask her what she was seeing?"

Jeannine shook her head and said, "No, my cousin Louise did." Jeannine's voice was thick with emotion as she continued. "You know what she said? She said that there was a beautiful light, and there were people: her brother, her father and mother, and her sister and lots of others. She said they had come to take her home.

"My cousin Louise got up into bed with my aunt Helen; she held her gently, rocking her, and said, 'It's okay, Momma, it's okay. We love you, but you can go with Grandpa and Grandma if you want.'"

Jeannine broke down in tears, tears that came from deep inside her heart.

In a broken voice Jeannine said, "Aunt Helen opened her eyes wide, and looking around the room, she whispered, 'Little Jean, come take Auntie's hand.' I walked over to the side of the bed, put her tiny hand in mine, and she smiled at me. In a gentle voice she said, 'Don't be afraid, little Jean. I'm not. It's beautiful where I'm going, so much love, so much love.'"

My eyes were filled with tears as I listened to Jeannine. I could see her frail little aunt lying there, face filled with that love she was talking about.

"Dawnea, she left her body a few minutes later. Smiling, she closed her eyes and went to join those people who were waiting to take her home."

I knelt beside Jeannine, hugging her. She smiled at me and said, "If I ever had any doubt about what you taught me, that experience affirmed that the Universe is about love. It was so beautiful."

*　　*　　*

Michel sat in front of me, waiting. He was such a lovely man, beautiful sculptured face, long golden hair, full lips. His wide green eyes were brimming with tears.

"Michel, are you ready to begin?"

In a heavy French accent he said, "Yes, yes, I am, Dawnea."

"Take a deep breath, hold it, let it go." As I took Michel through his circular breathing, the soundtrack to *Somewhere in Time* softly played in the background.

"See a giant screen in your mind, Michel." I guided him through the phasing, saying, "See someone coming through the clearing."

He gasped. "It's Henri. Oh, he is so beautiful. He is not sick anymore, he is well. He is so at peace. He is reaching out to me."

"Take his hand, Michel. Embrace him. Let him speak to you. Feel his love for you."

"He is telling me he is in a place where there is no pain, no suffering, where there is no AIDS. Oh, there are others, there is my friend John." Excitedly he continued. "Eric, looking so strong, so many of my friends are here with Henri."

Tears streamed down Michel's face, spilling into his long hair. "There is no suffering in this place. Dawnea, it is wonderful, so beautiful."

Michel was very still. His face was radiant.

"Michel, when you are ready, allow the screen to disappear. Open your eyes, be present, be in the now."

I waited for Michel to open his eyes.

His face was radiant, peaceful. He was awed. He told me, "Dawnea, it was so beautiful, I did not want to leave. Henri was as he was when we first became lovers, before the AIDS ravaged his body. He is that way now, I know it. I know, I saw him, I felt him. I could smell his cologne. He looked so alive, so sensual. But . . . it is also sad."

"Tell me, Michel."

He started to cry, saying, "So many, I saw so many around him. All who were beautiful, but all died of AIDS." He shook his head and stated, "What a waste."

Tears filled my own eyes as I thought back on the people I had worked on who had that disease. "Michel," I gently said, "I know nothing can really ease the pain of Henri's loss. But think about this: He is in a beautiful place. He is surrounded by love. And his body is free of suffering." I stood up from my chair, knelt down beside Michel, and took his hand as I continued. "Can we rejoice together that he has found his way home?"

Michel smiled through his tears as we hugged each other tightly.

If you have a loved one who has passed over to the Spirit Side and you have unanswered feelings, unanswered questions, use this phase. Use that screen in your mind, allow your emotions to flood you—and just let it rip. Allow the healing to begin.

Every day of our lives, if we will just open to it, the

Divine Spark within will fill us with that love. And when we have that love we can trust, we can open and share it with others. We don't have to wait until we leave our bodies. We can have that love, that radiant light, every single moment of every day.

GIVING BACK

Our world is crying,
Crying desperate cries for healing.
The trees are weeping,
The oceans are bleeding.
Even the rocks cry out in despairing anguish.
And the souls that live on this planet,
Oh, those sweet souls,
Each one cries for a healing.
For a release from the pain.
We can give it,
Each one of us can send it out there . . .
Send the love.

"The Circle"
by Dawnea Adams

In my Intraphase workshops, at the end of the day, when we'd worked so hard on healing our own lives, I would ask the group to join hands and give that love back, back to the world we live in.

That's what I'm asking of you right now. See that giant screen in your mind. See all the people of the earth—every race, every creed, every color—see all of us joining hands to heal this planet.

The healing starts within each one of us. Each time we have a victory over the scars of our past, over our pain, each time we allow that Divine Spark within us to ignite, that energy goes out into the world.

So, now see each person on our planet with their Divine Spark ignited. See us all living the love.

SO BE IT!!!

PLAY IT AGAIN, SAM

〜

Okay, so you've tried phasing and you say, "I can't quite get it, Dawnea. I read about the other people you worked with. Well, the earth and heavens did not move for me."

To begin with, from this second on, do not compare yourself with *anyone* else ever again. The people in this book are real people, with real-life pain, trying to scale their mountains and slay their dragons—just like you. If phasing isn't working for you, read on.

1. When you are soul surfing through each phasing technique, be *honest* with yourself. Choose the phase that will most help you remove any debris standing in the way of the phase that will get you the "goodies."

If you do not follow this guideline, you will find yourself distracted, unfocused. It's like when you were little and you had homework. If you sneaked outside to play, it wasn't really that much fun. You knew you had that homework waiting for you. So do your inner homework first, that is, "You do the work, you get the goodies."

2. After your intuition has chosen the phase, have you read it over and over? Is it absolutely clear to you what you are doing and *why* you are doing it?

If there is any hesitation at all, you are not ready. Read it again, go out and rent the movie on video that relates to that phase. Get your songs out. You must have your emotions and heart connected to what you are doing. Otherwise, you are just going through the motion of having emotions. You will get nowhere. Remember: Imagination, Intuition, and Emotion are the key buzzwords.

3. Go back into your childhood when you were nine or ten years old. What were your daydreams like? What did you want to be when you grew up? At that age you still had an imagination. If necessary, go back there. Dig it up out of the archives in your mind. Dust it off and start phasing.

4. This is a must. You must connect your emotions to what you are phasing. Just like when you go to the movies. Do you sit there and think about feeling? Hell, no. You just go with what is happening on that screen. This is what I want you to do here. Go with what is on that screen in your mind. Do not allow your old conditioning to get in the way. Just keep on phasing; you will feel it, it will kick in. Once it does, you will feel the connection with your heart, with your emotions. That is the juice that feeds the part of your brain that makes things happen. It feeds your subconscious.

Have you done the preproduction work? Set the scene, choosing the musical score, set the mood in the room. I know this might all sound a little weird, but once again, we are feeding the subconscious new experiences, so setting up the scene before you shoot the movie (phase) is essential. In addition to the music, the lights are great scene setters, especially candles. Even the smells are important. All of these things feed your emotions, and your emotions are what feed the subconscious. Let me repeat what I said at the beginning of the book: The subconscious mind does not know the difference between "real-life" experience and phasing. *If* the emotions are working, the subconscious mind will get it, and then so will you—out there in your life, in the world outside of phasing, the world of your day-to-day life. In the beginning this is a must. After a while you'll get so good at this, you will do it walking down the street or driving in your car. But for starters, concentrate on the techniques until you see that phasing does work. You will know that it works because you will see the results in your life. Results are what we are after here. Stop doubting and get to work!!!

Rock and Roll!!!